Adult Coloring Book

An array of Mandela's from this one Drawing

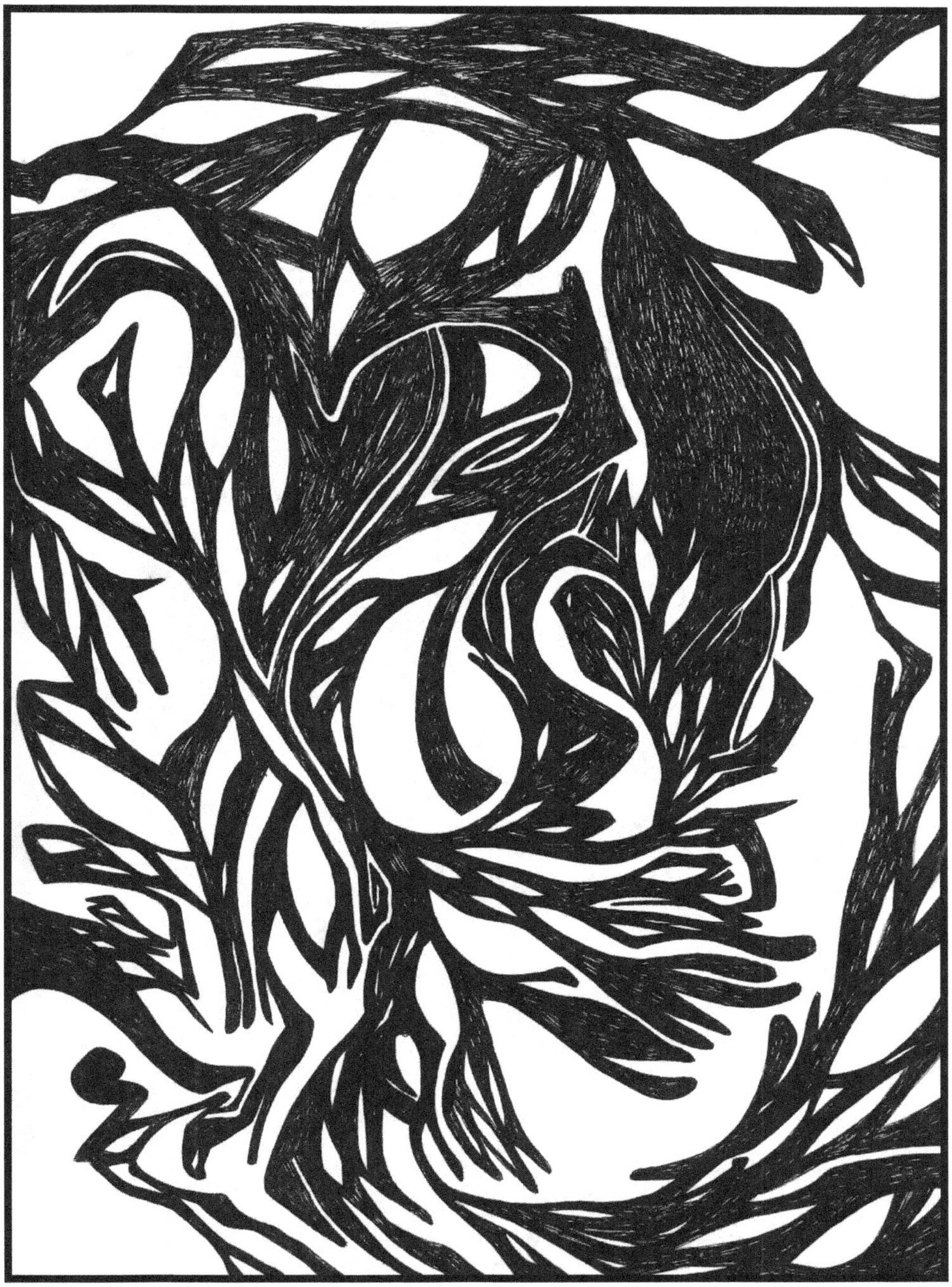

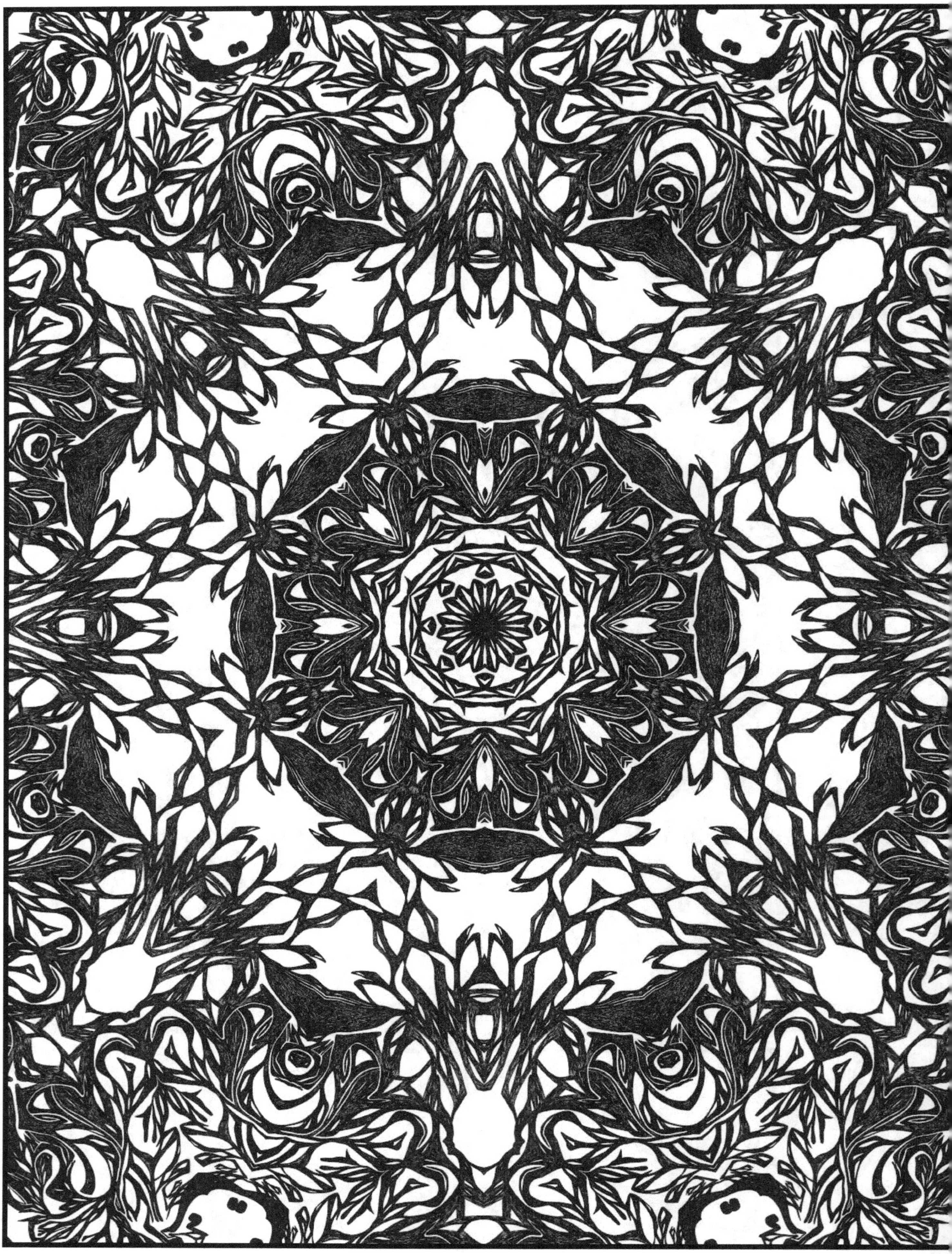

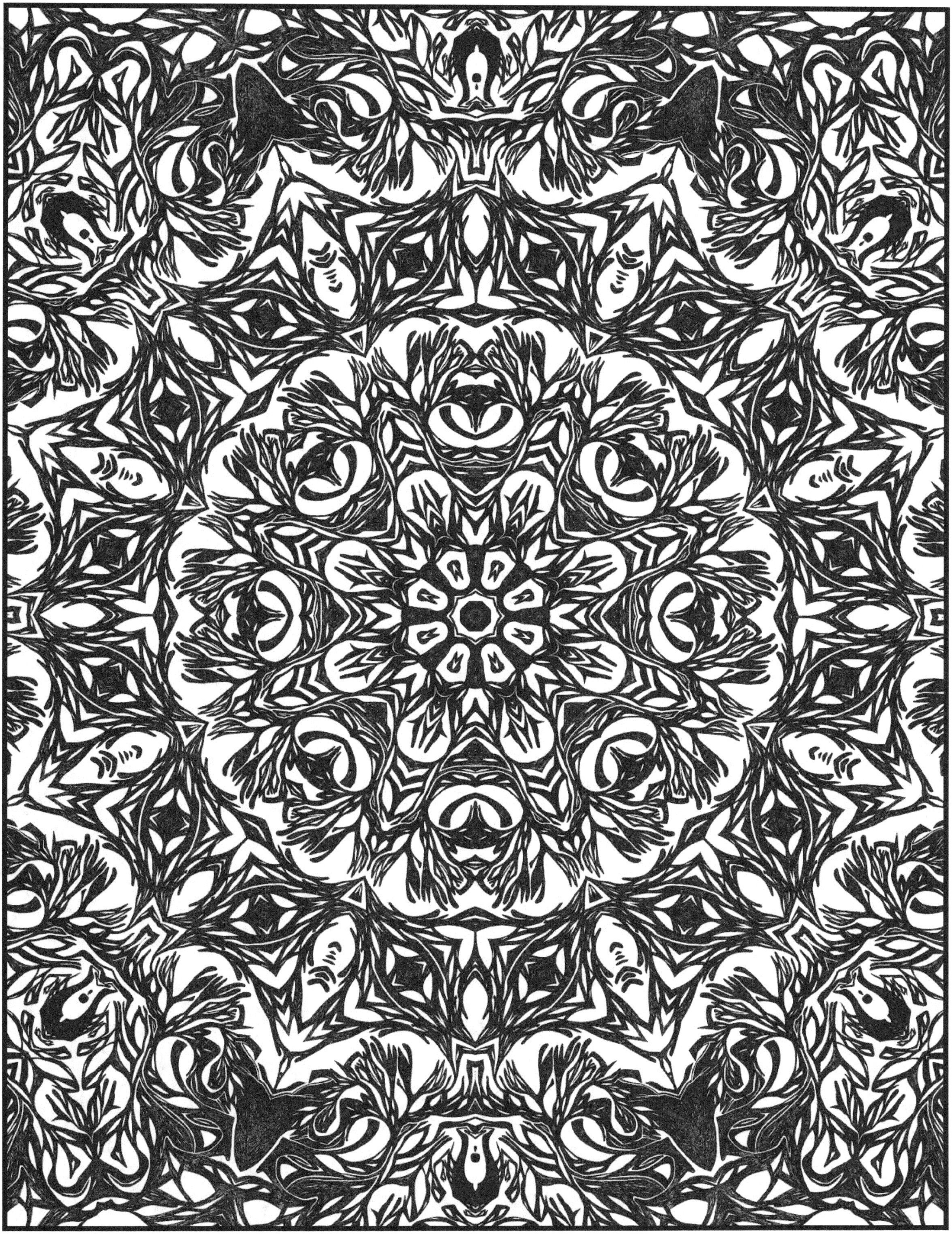

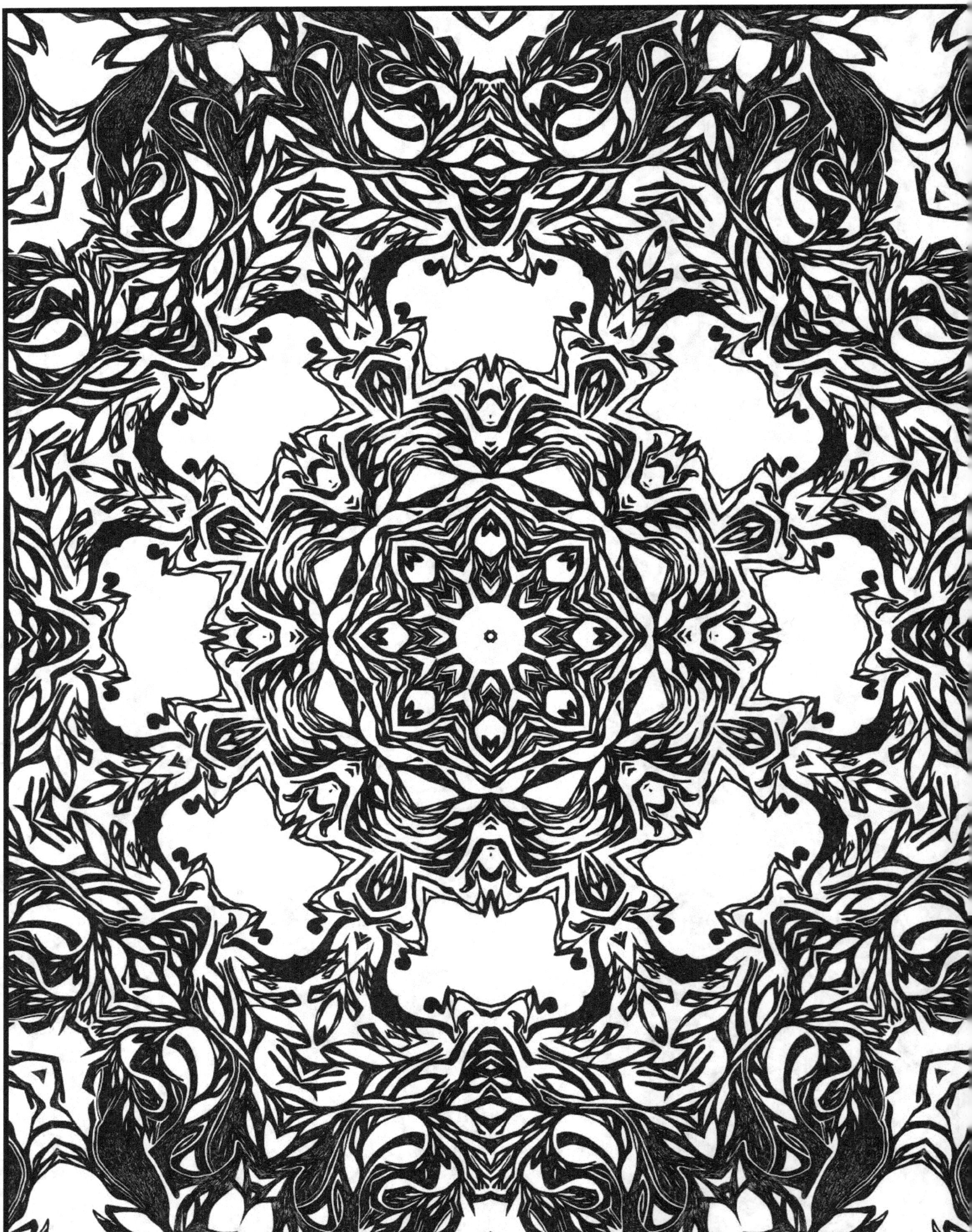

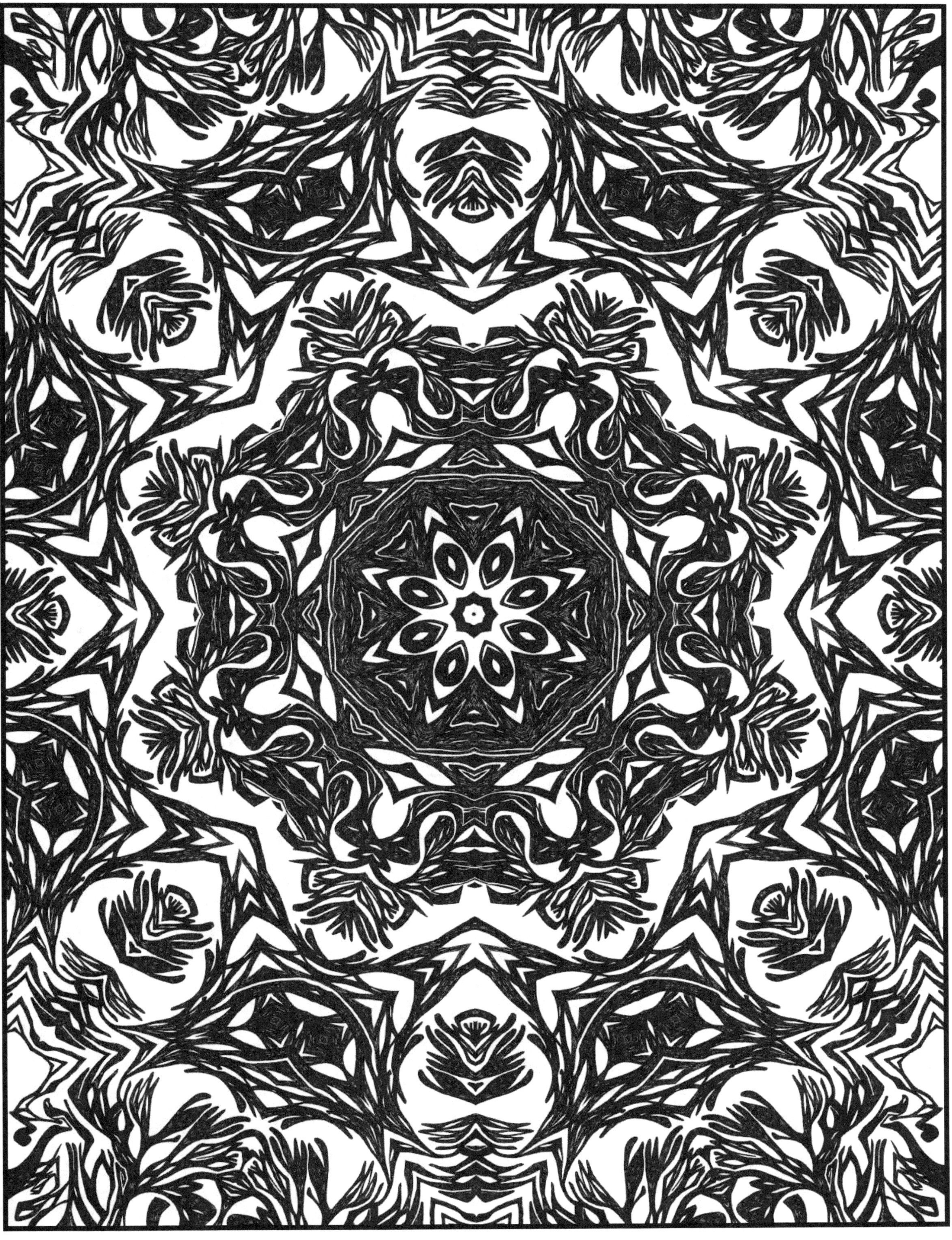

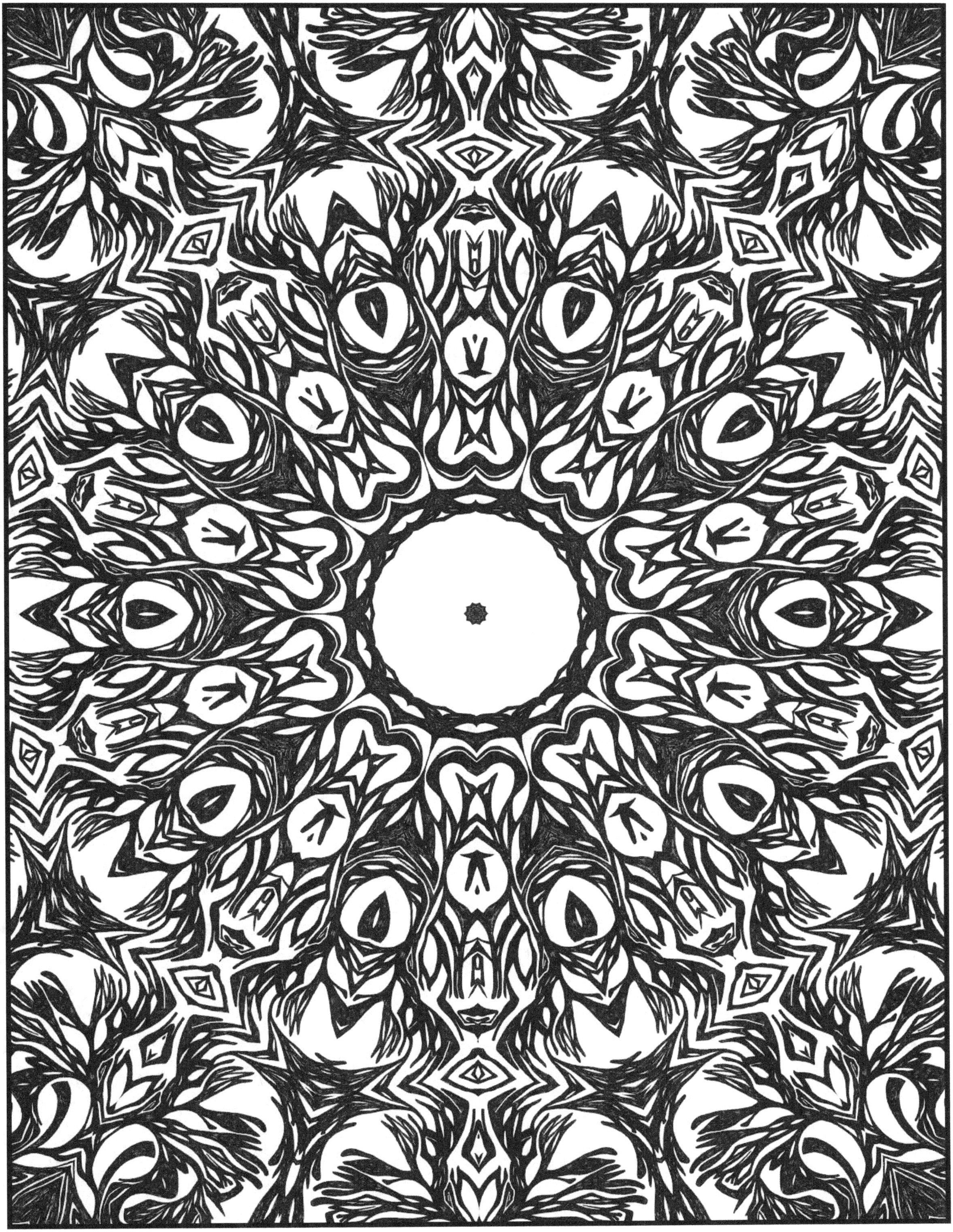

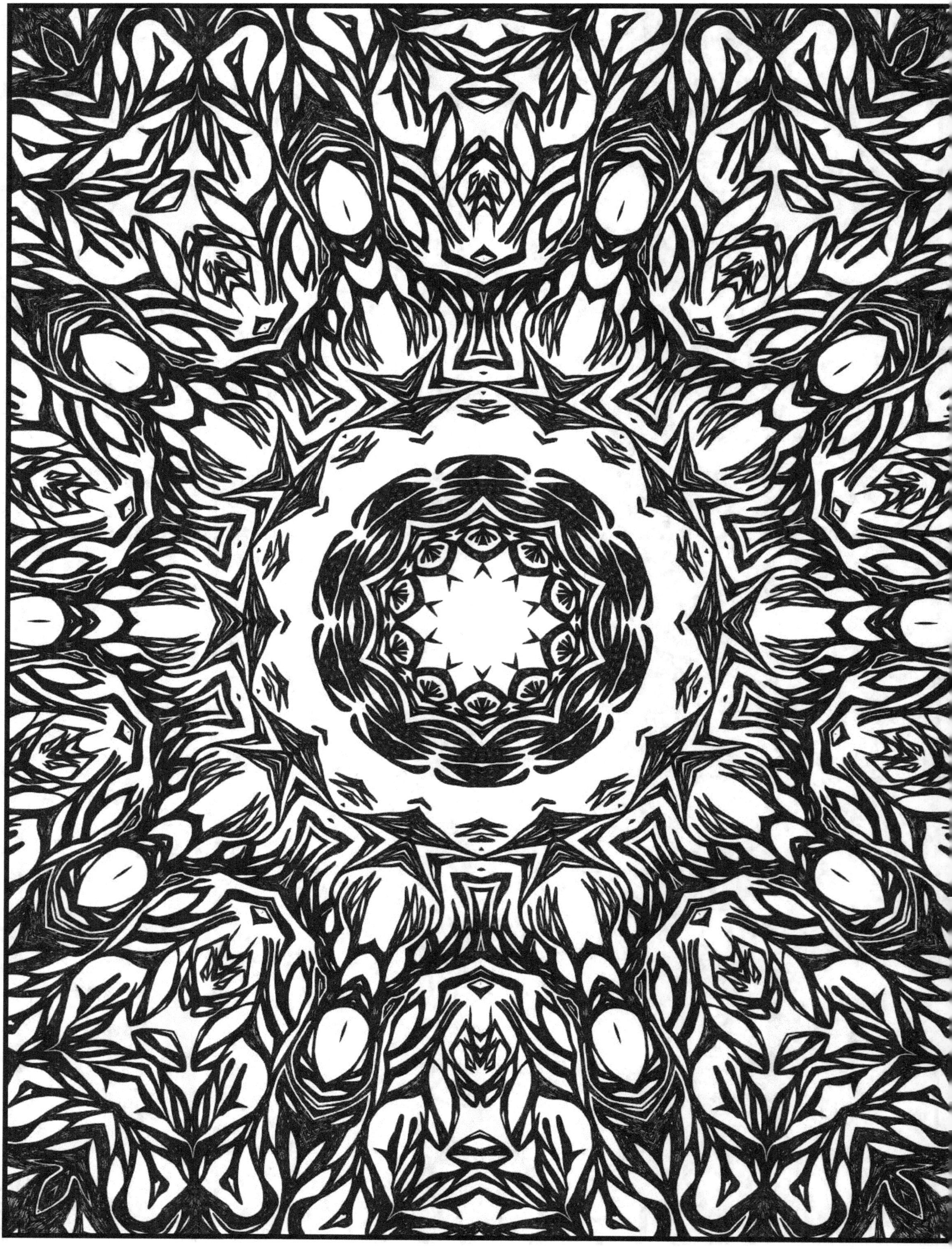

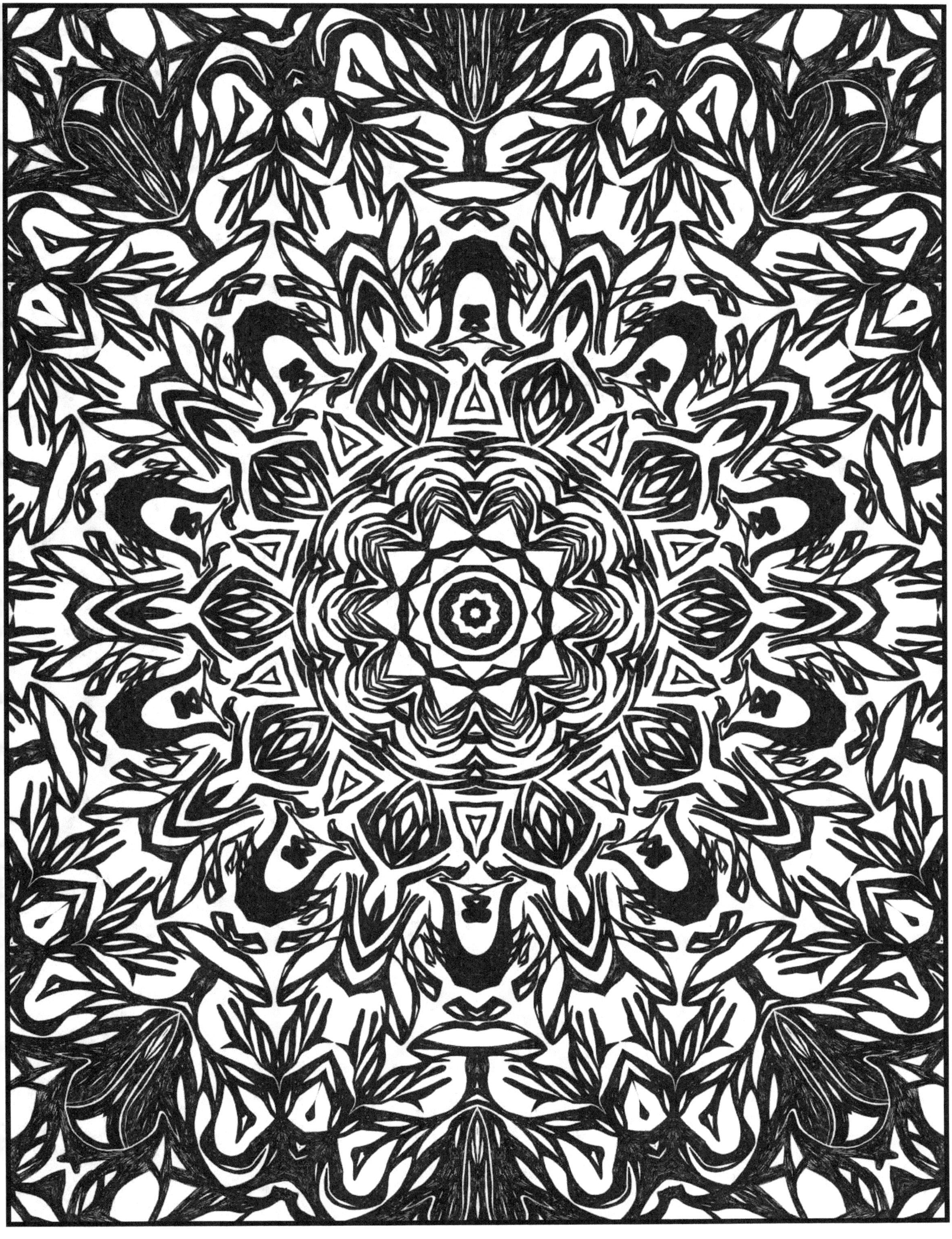

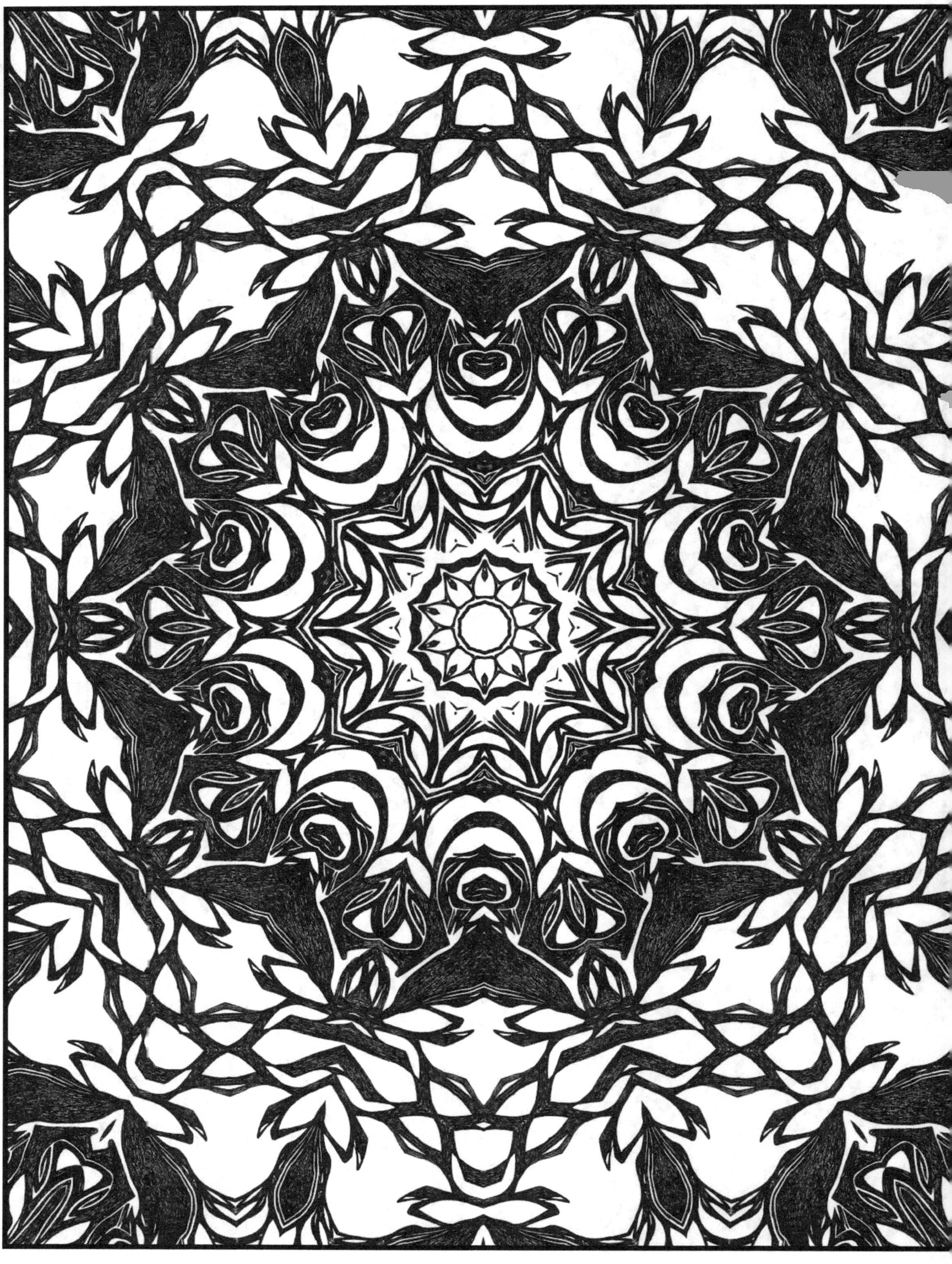

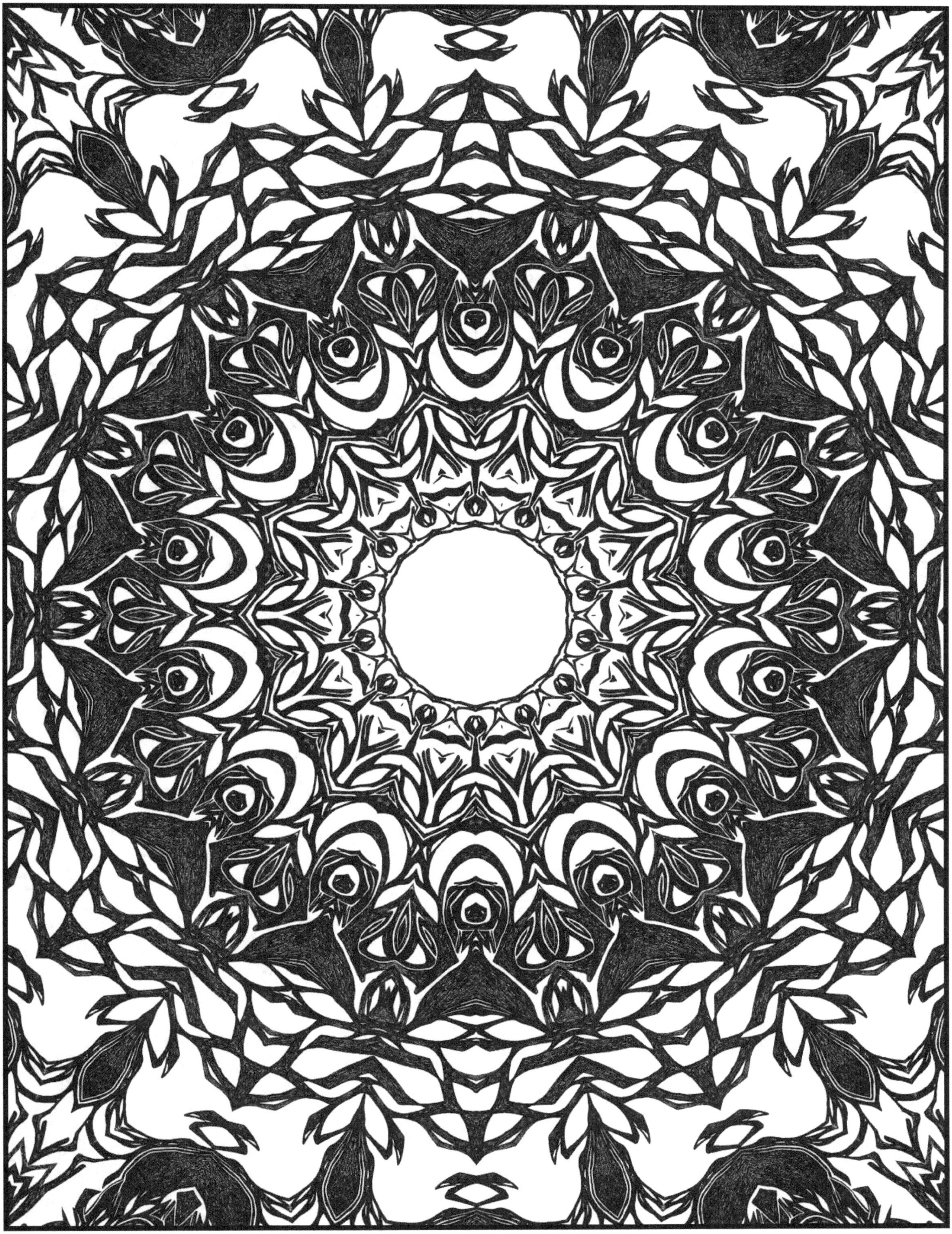

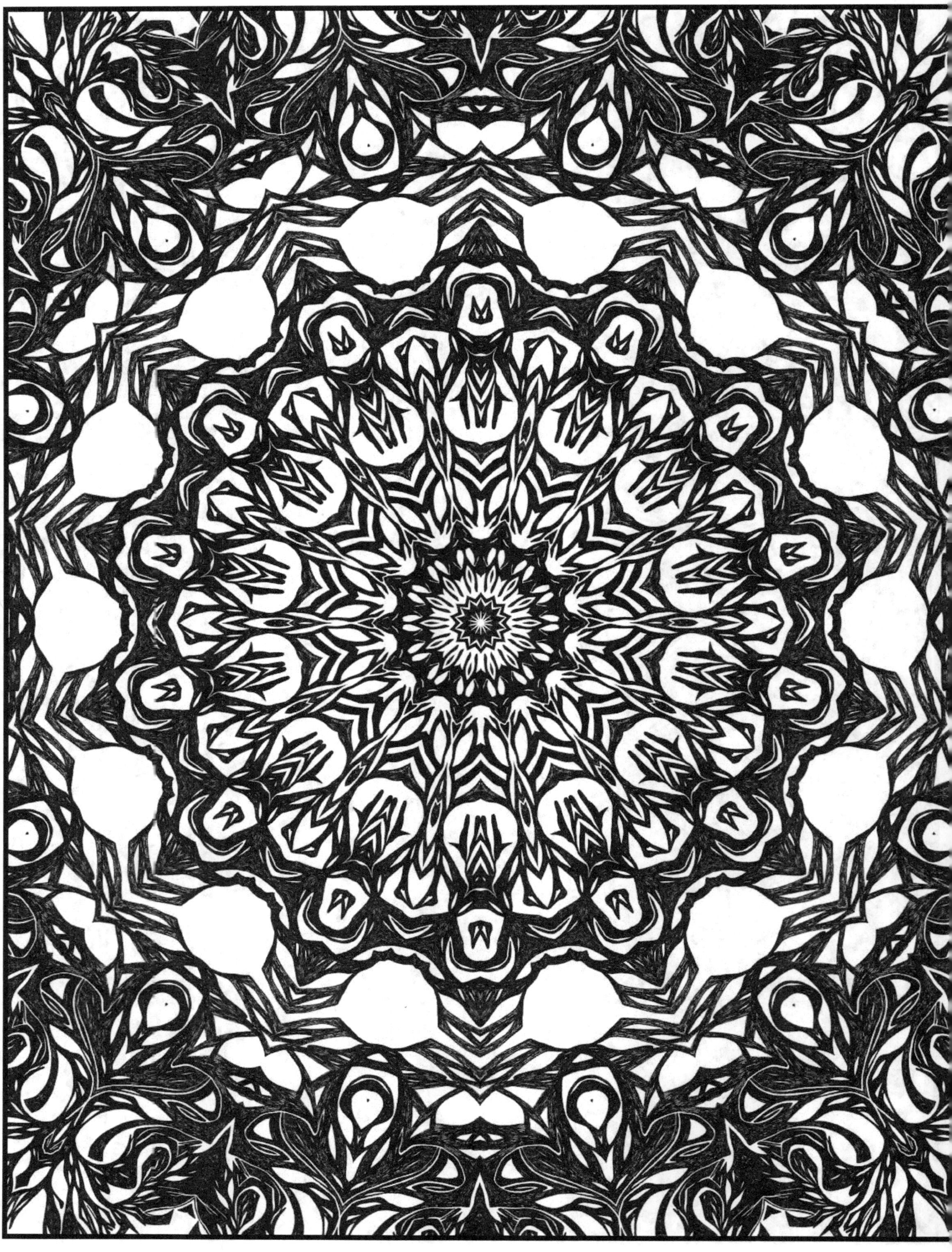

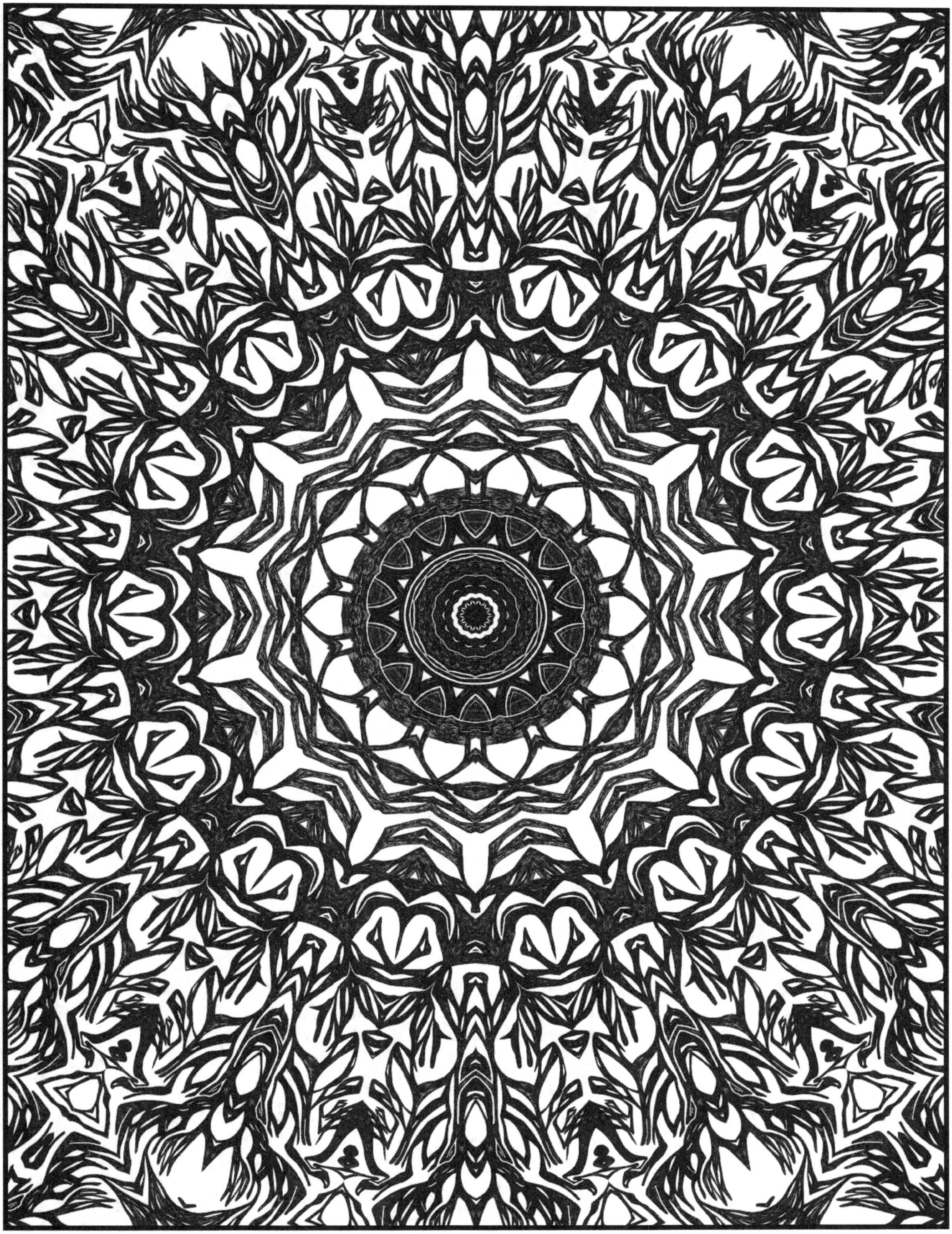

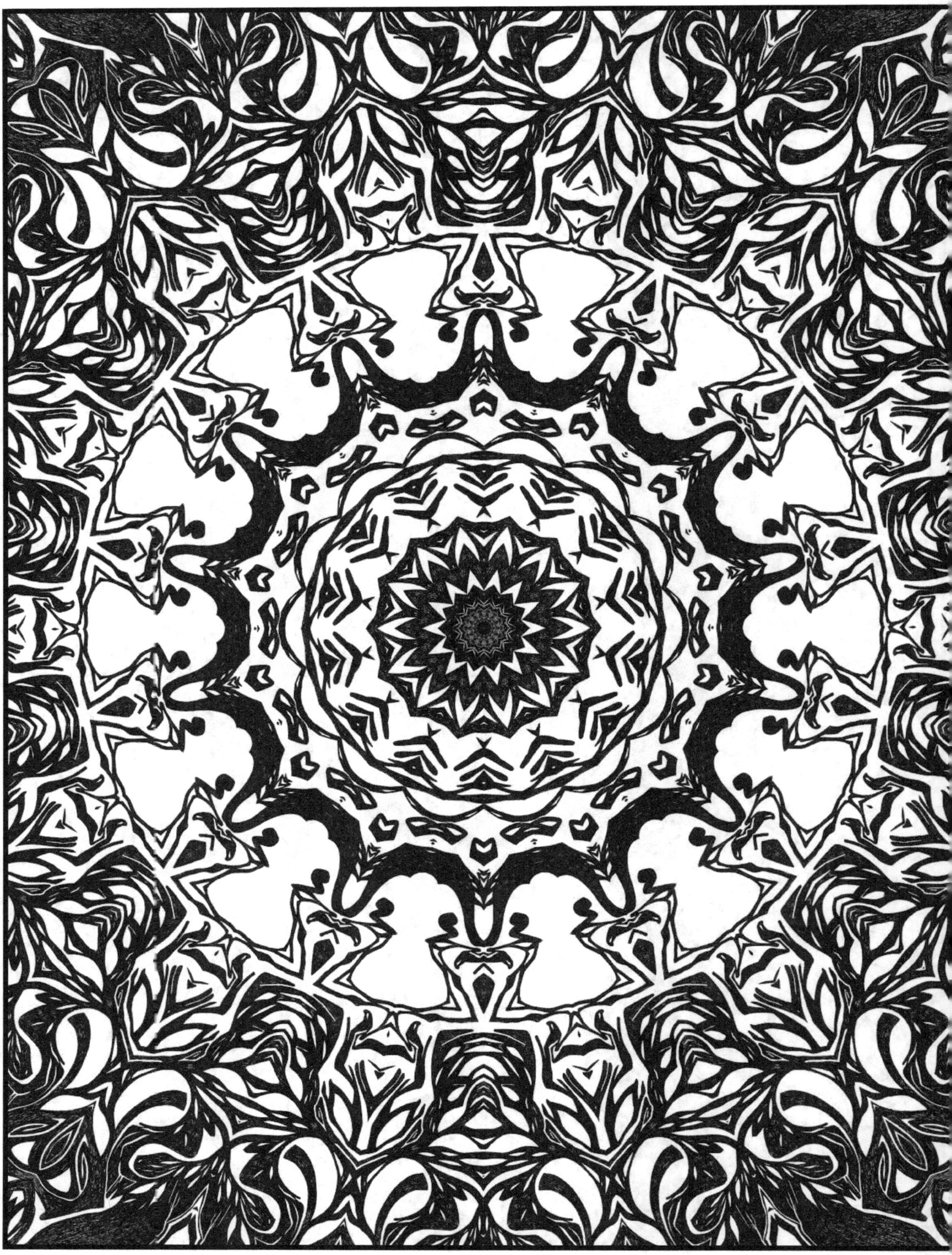

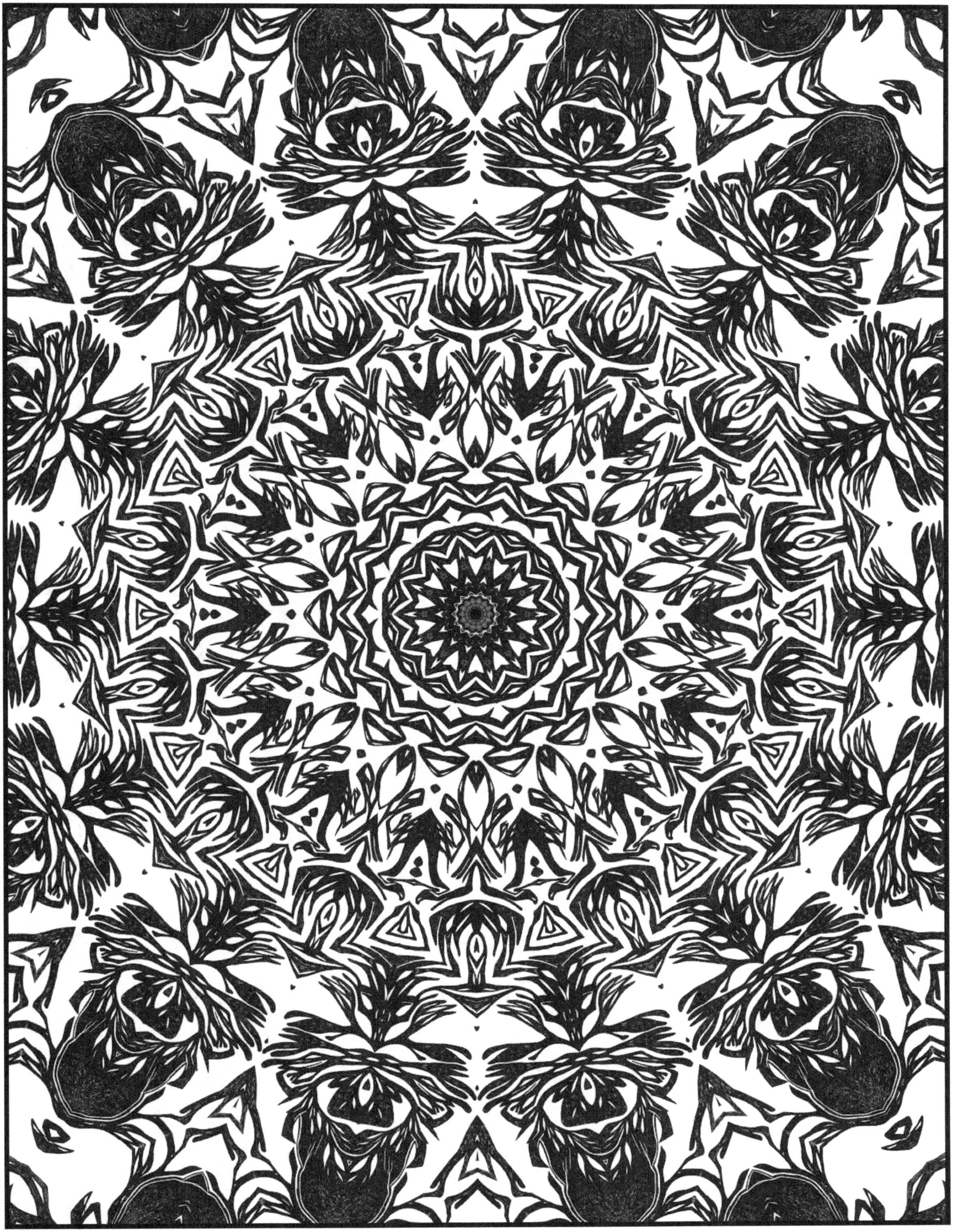

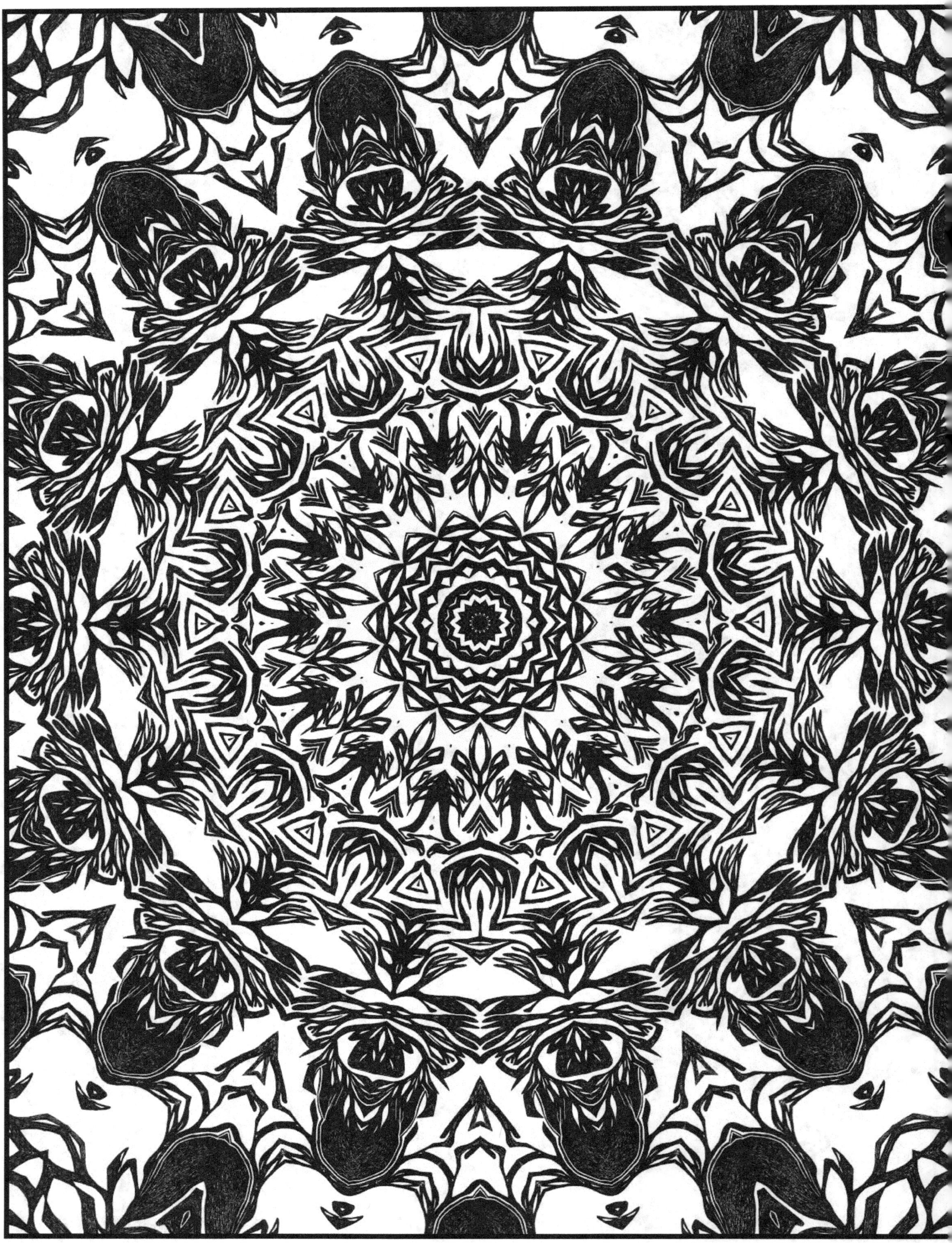

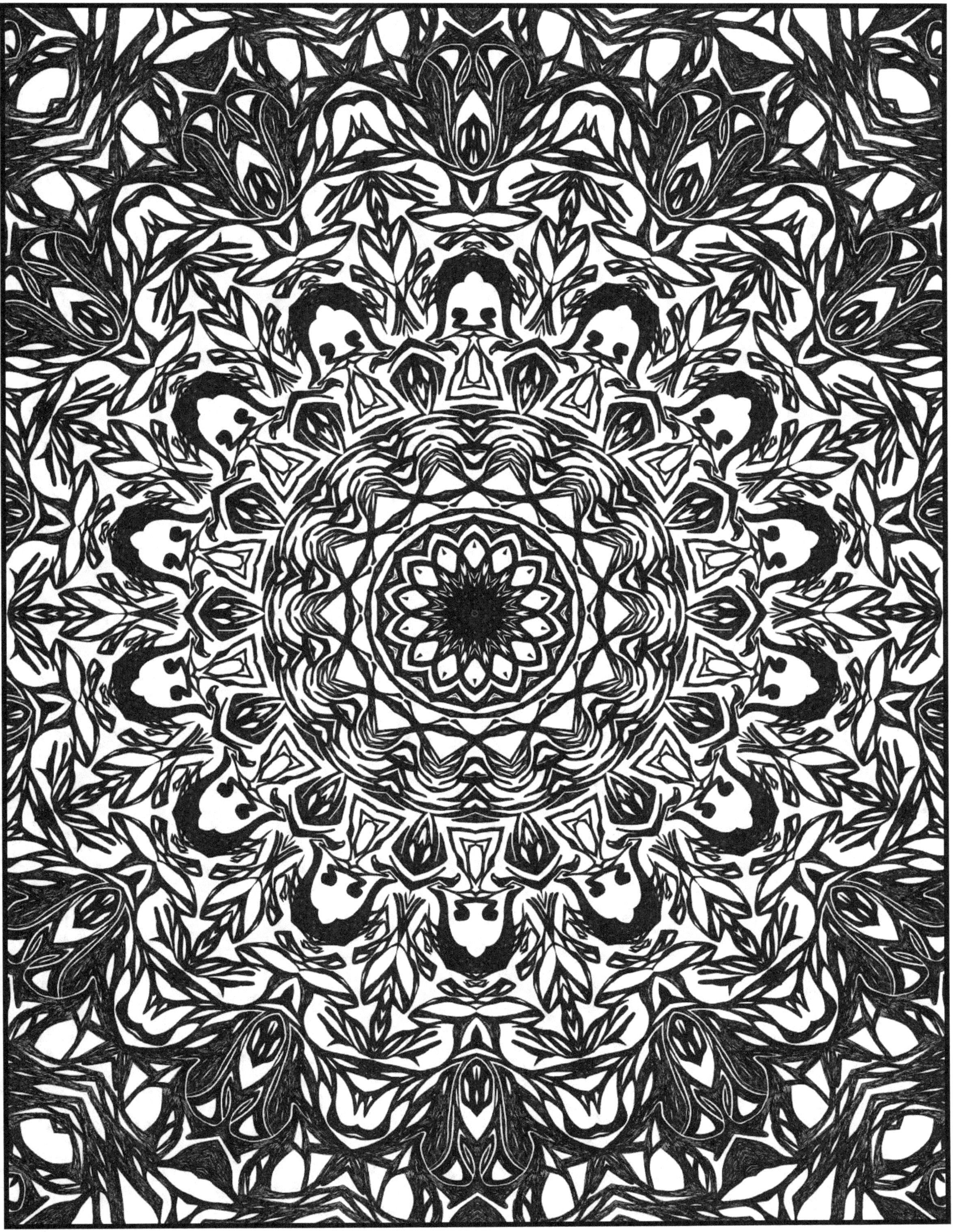

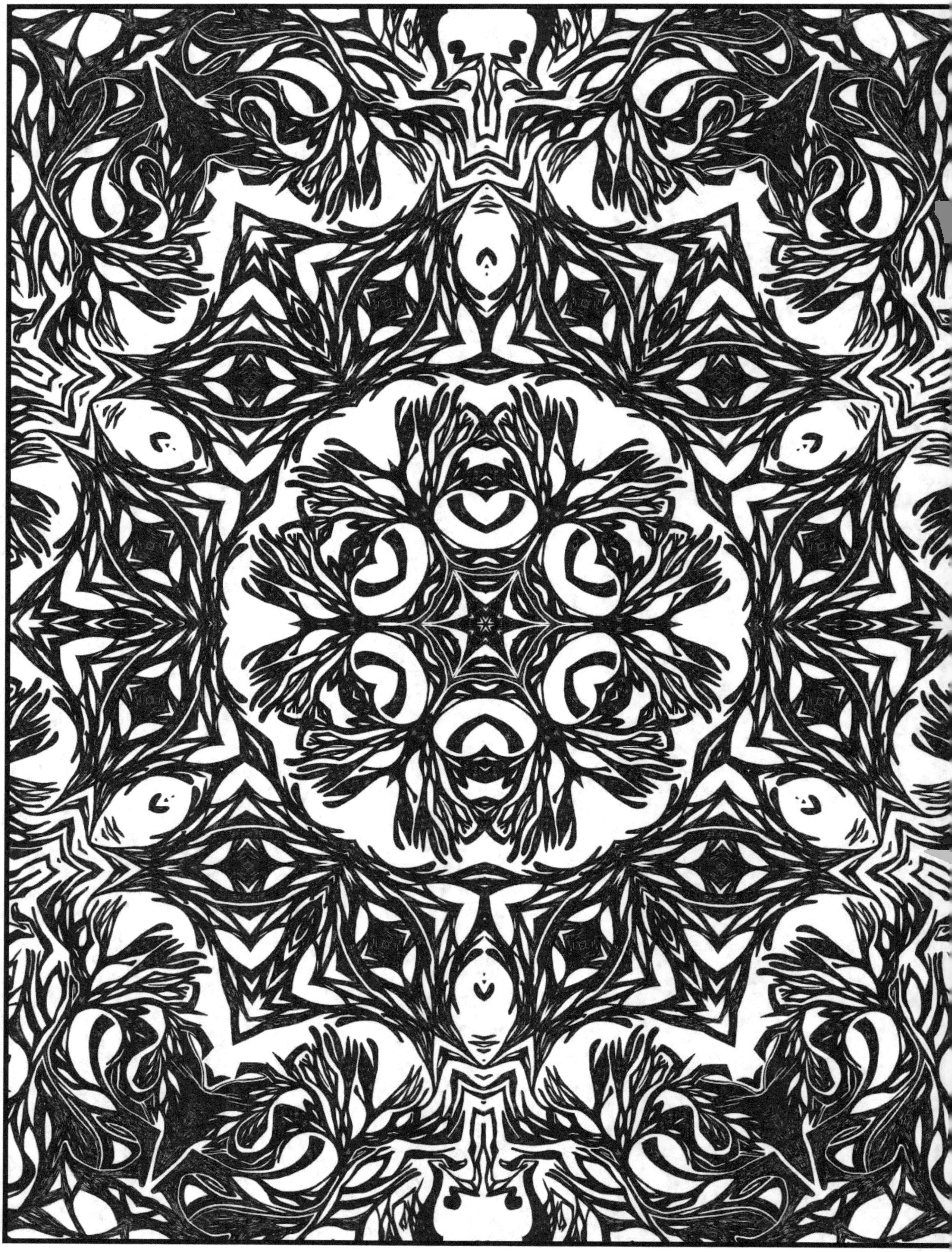

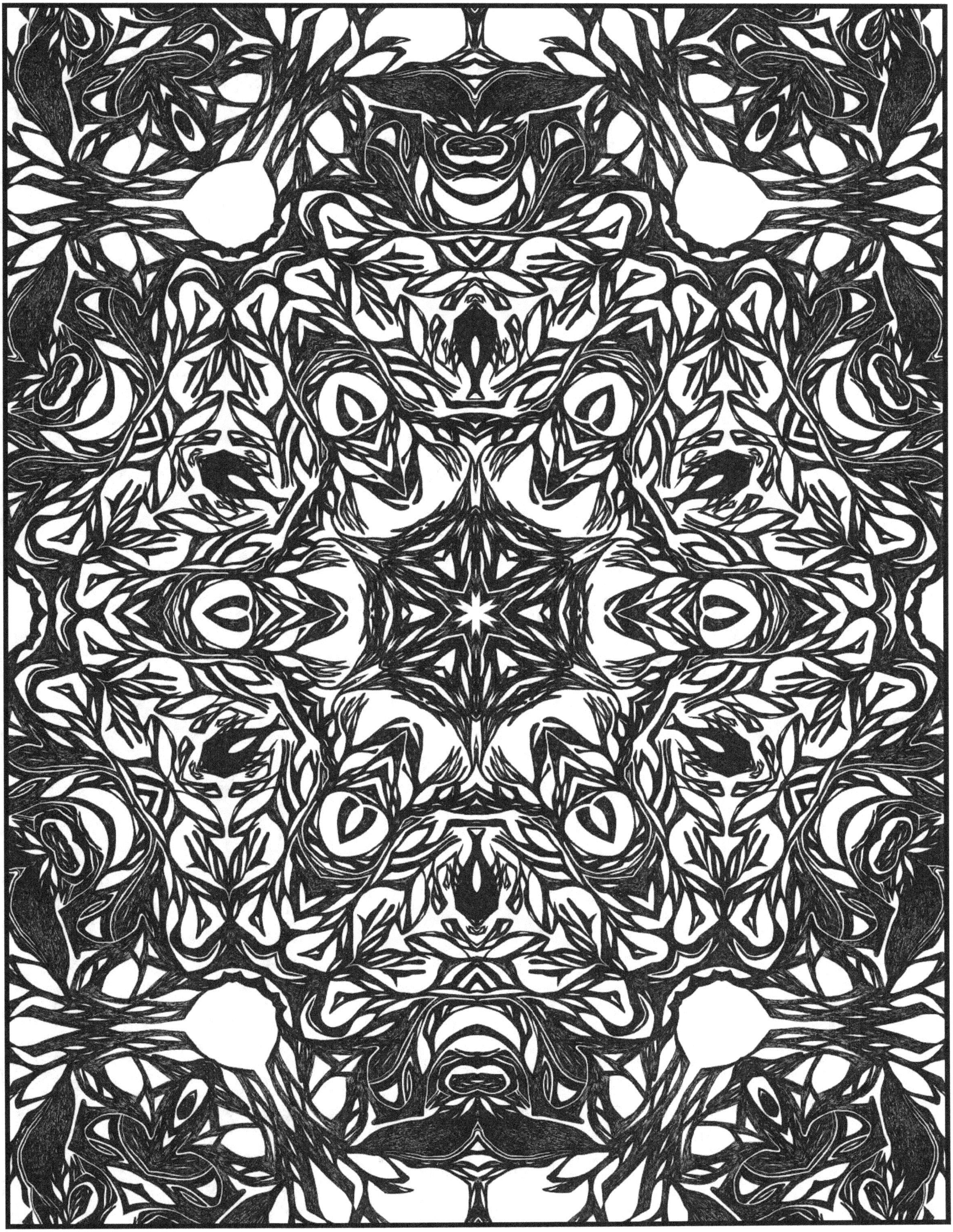

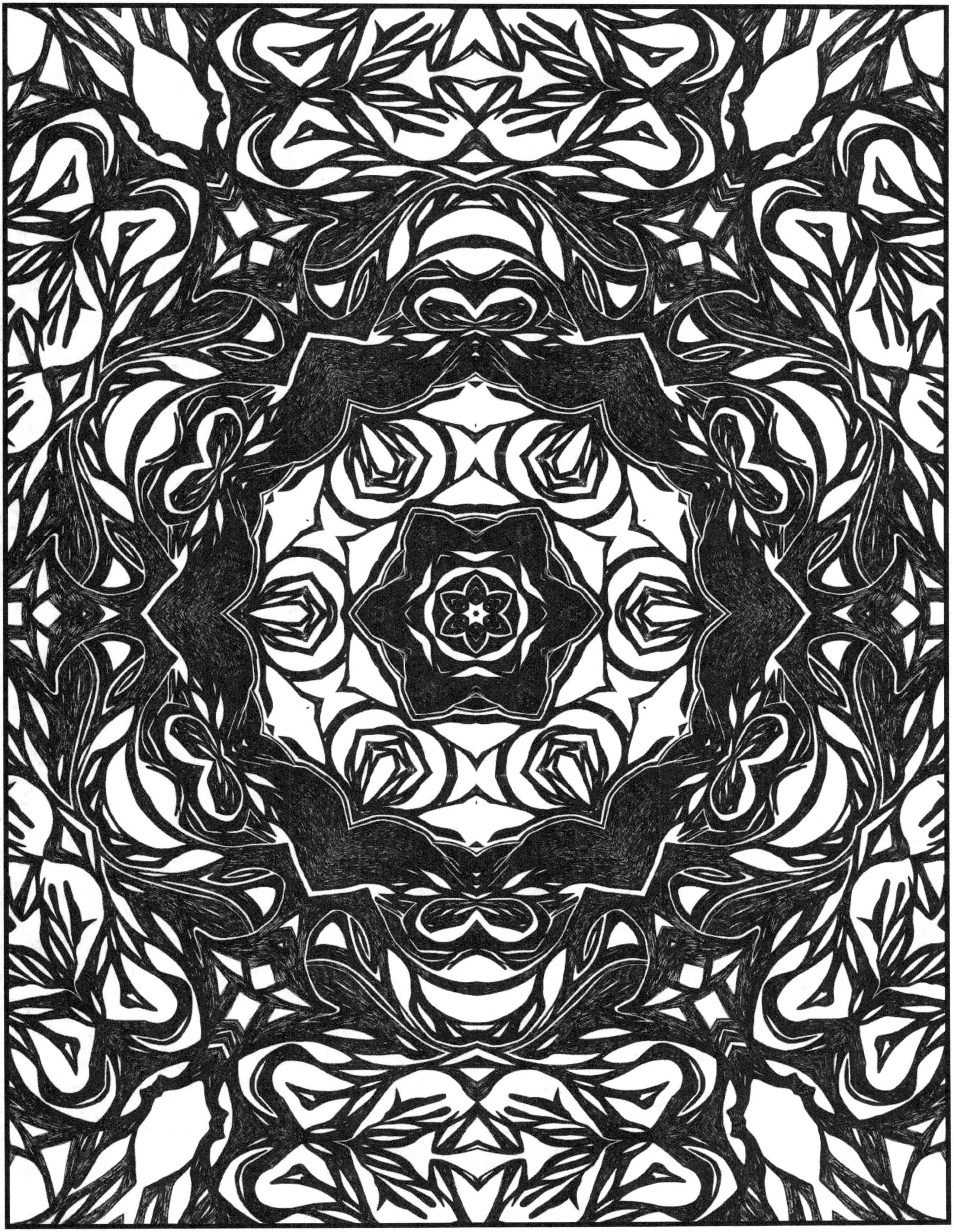

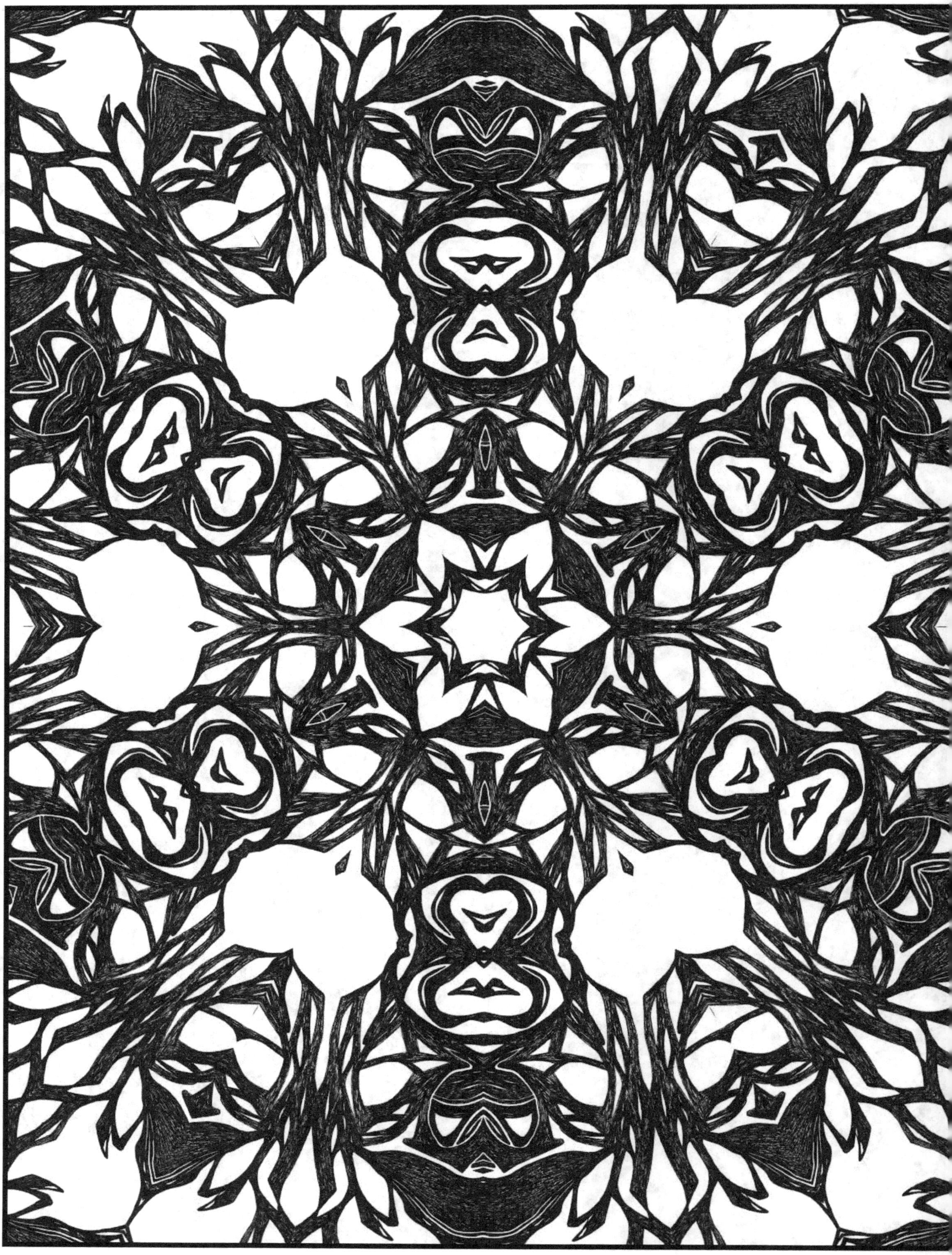

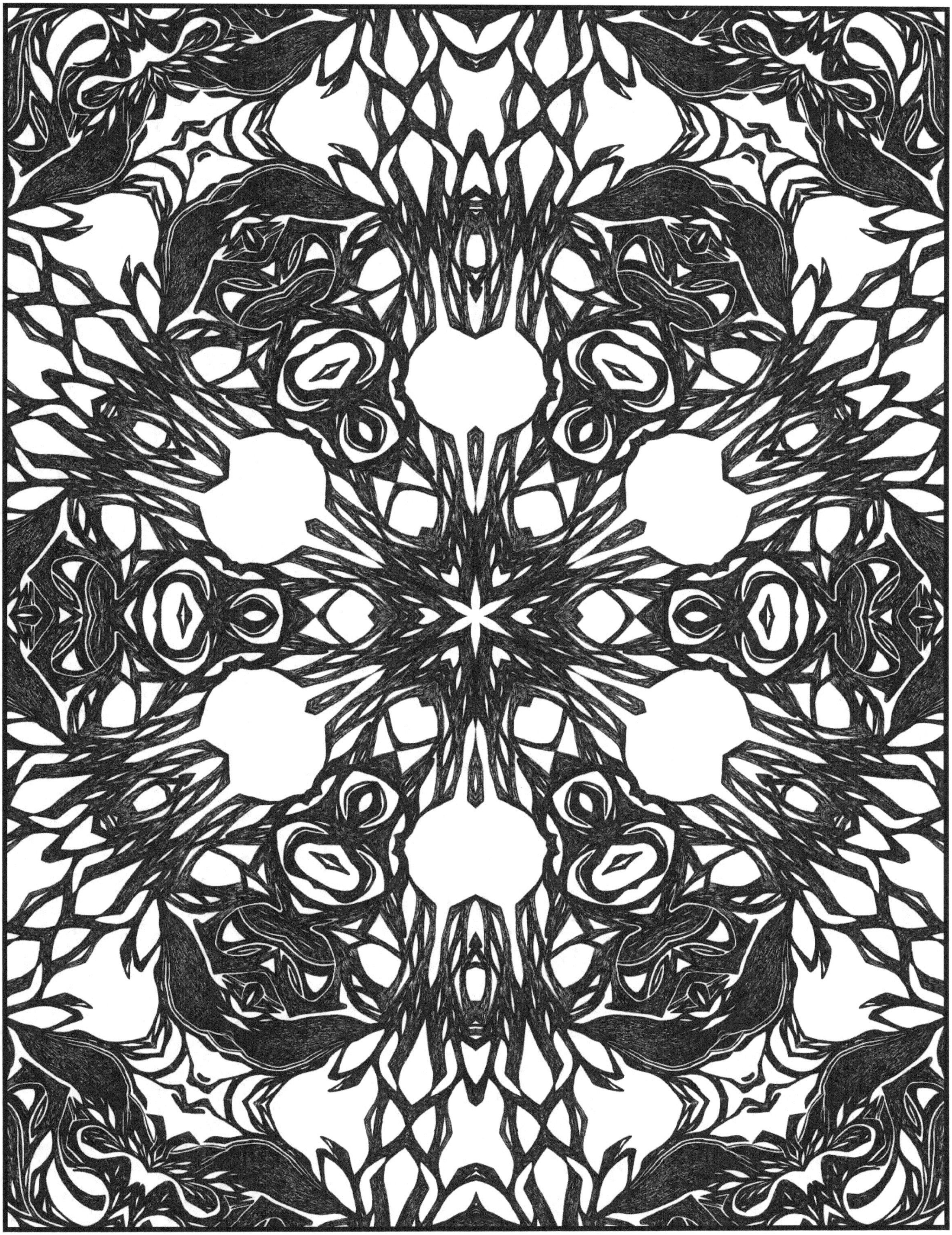

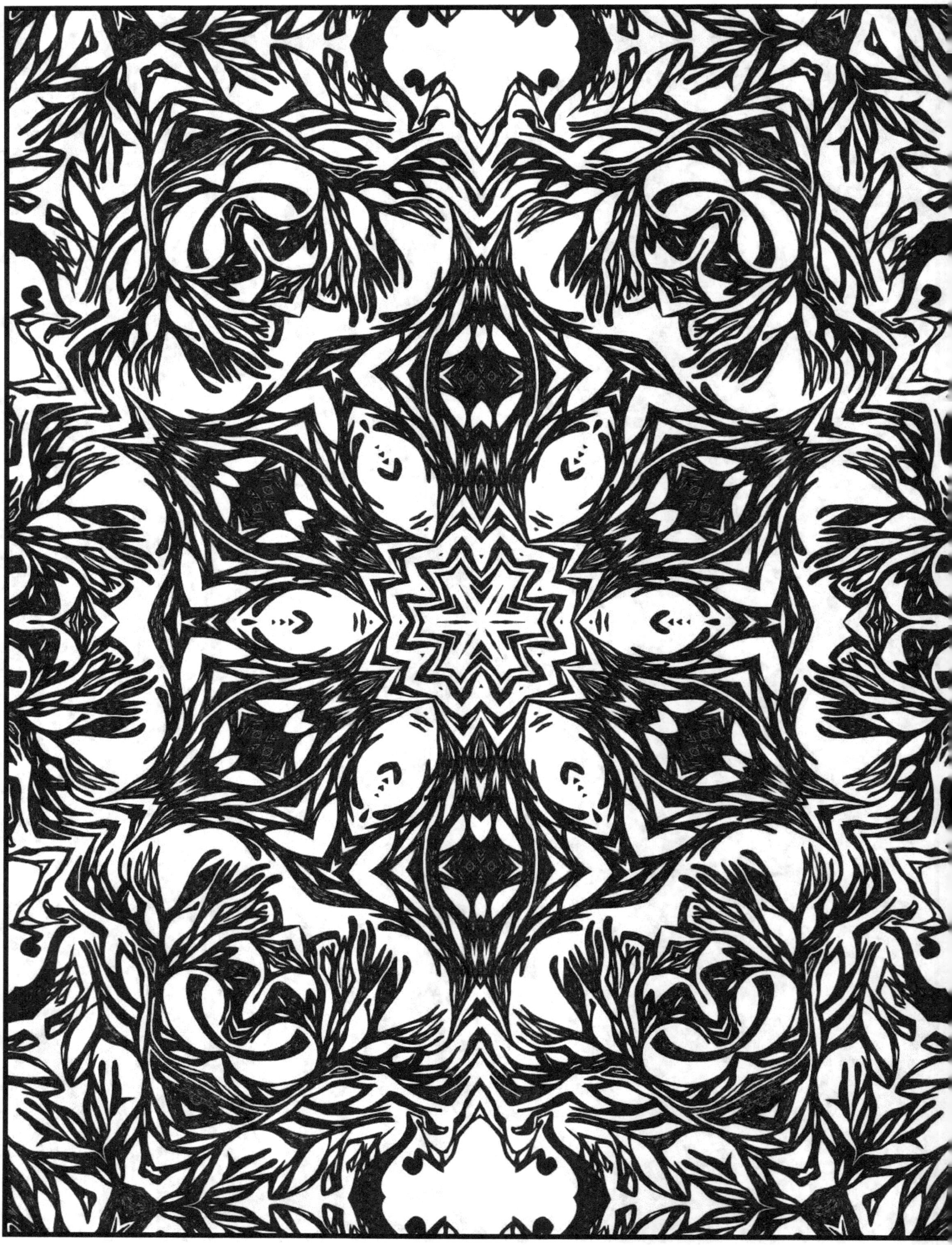

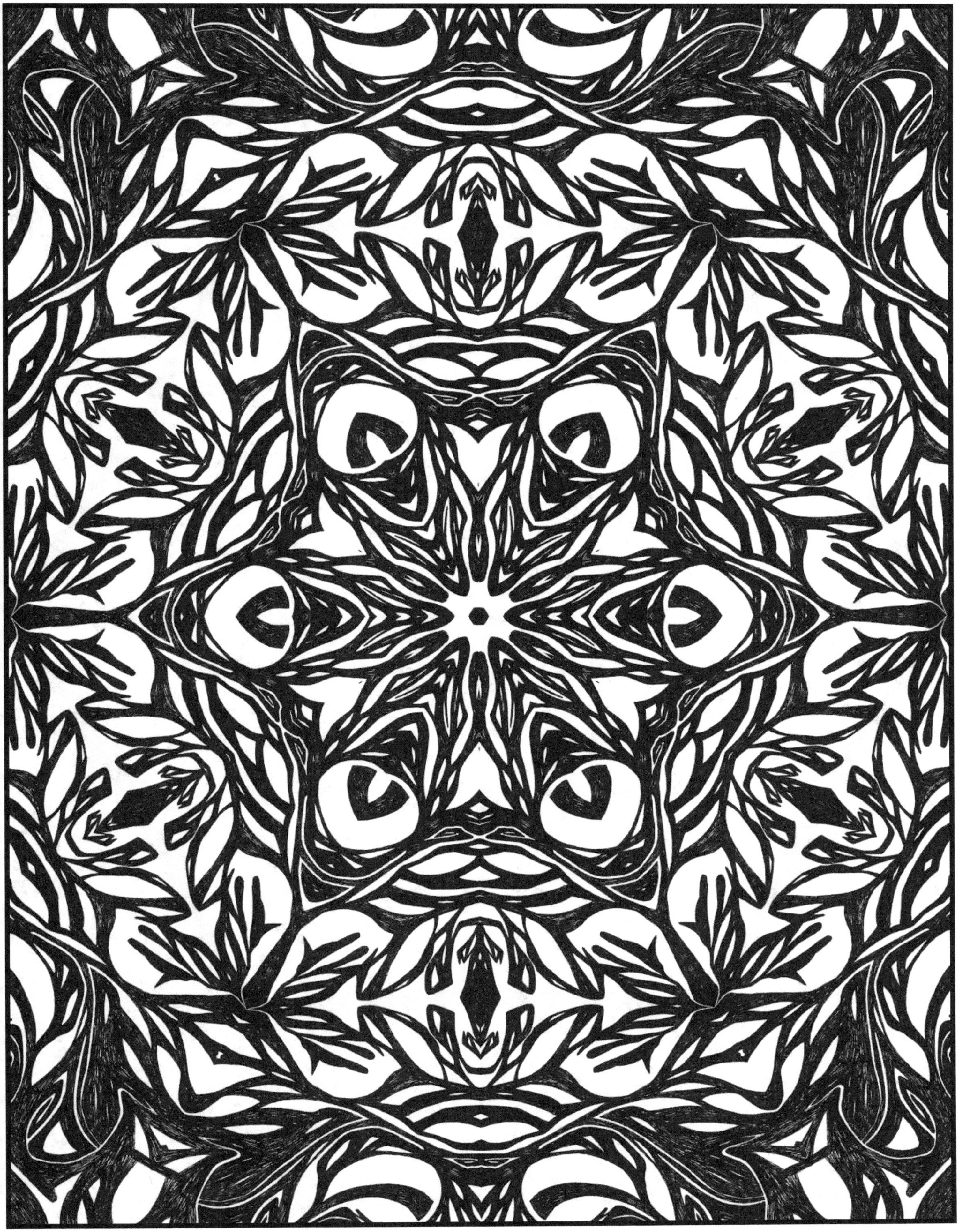

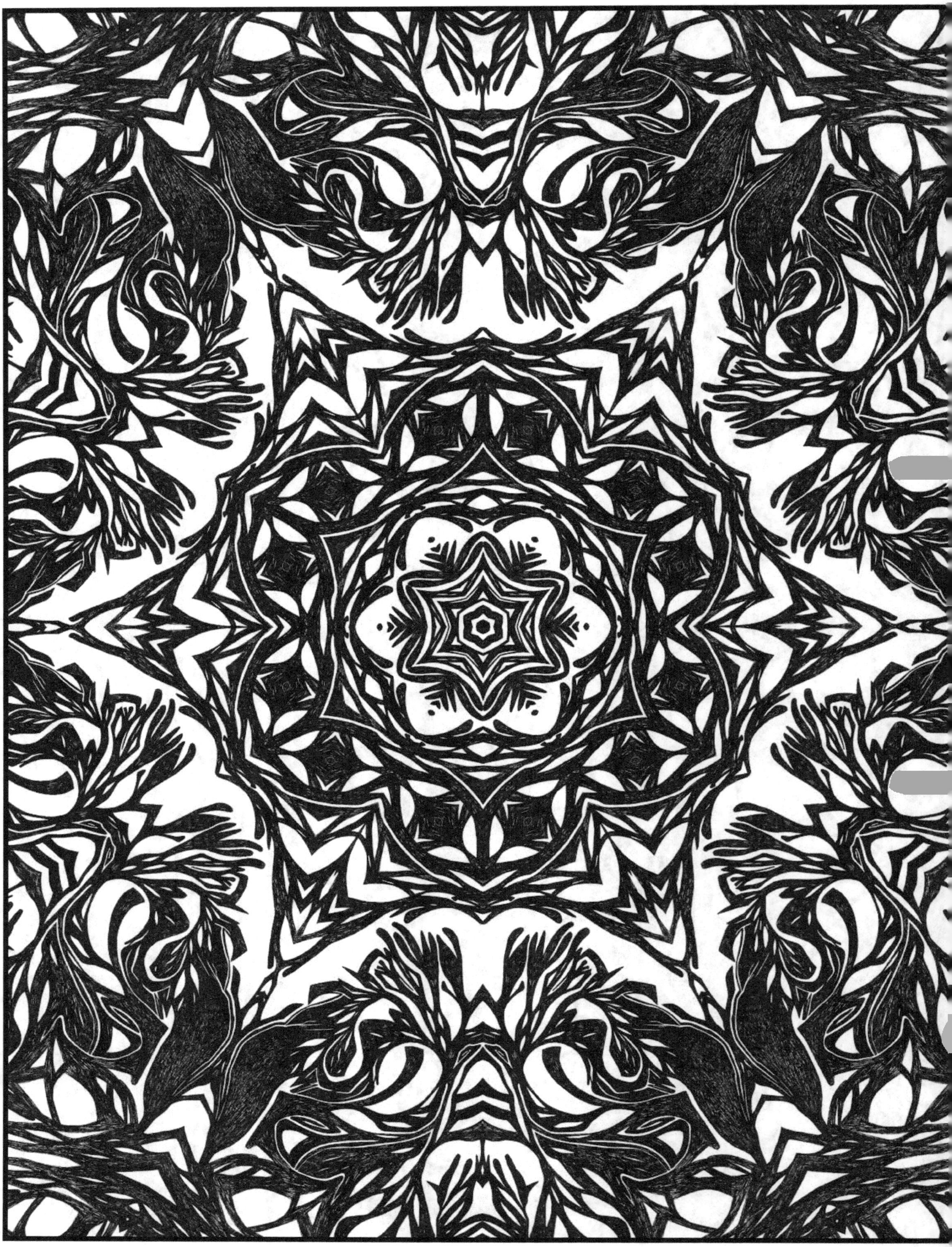

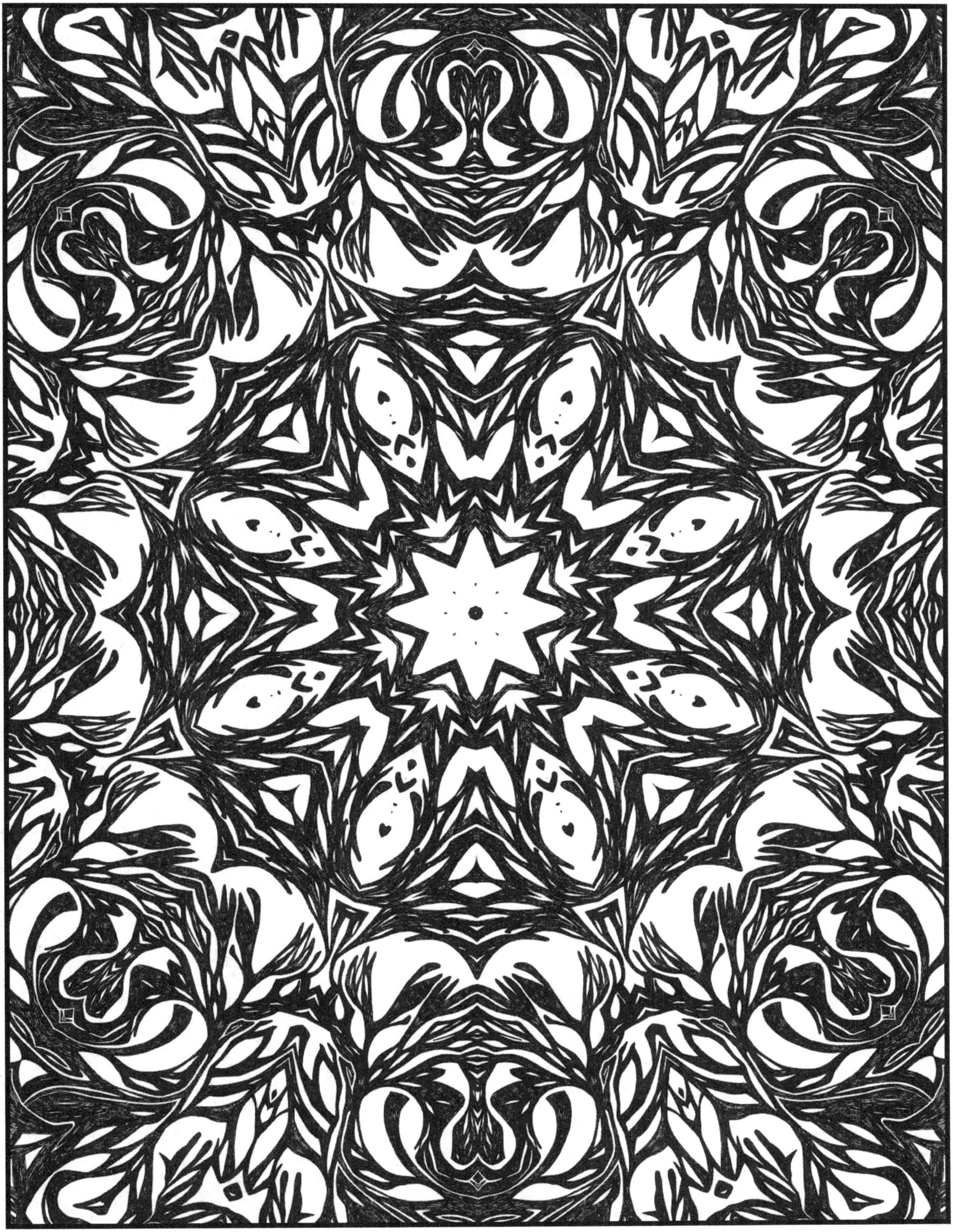

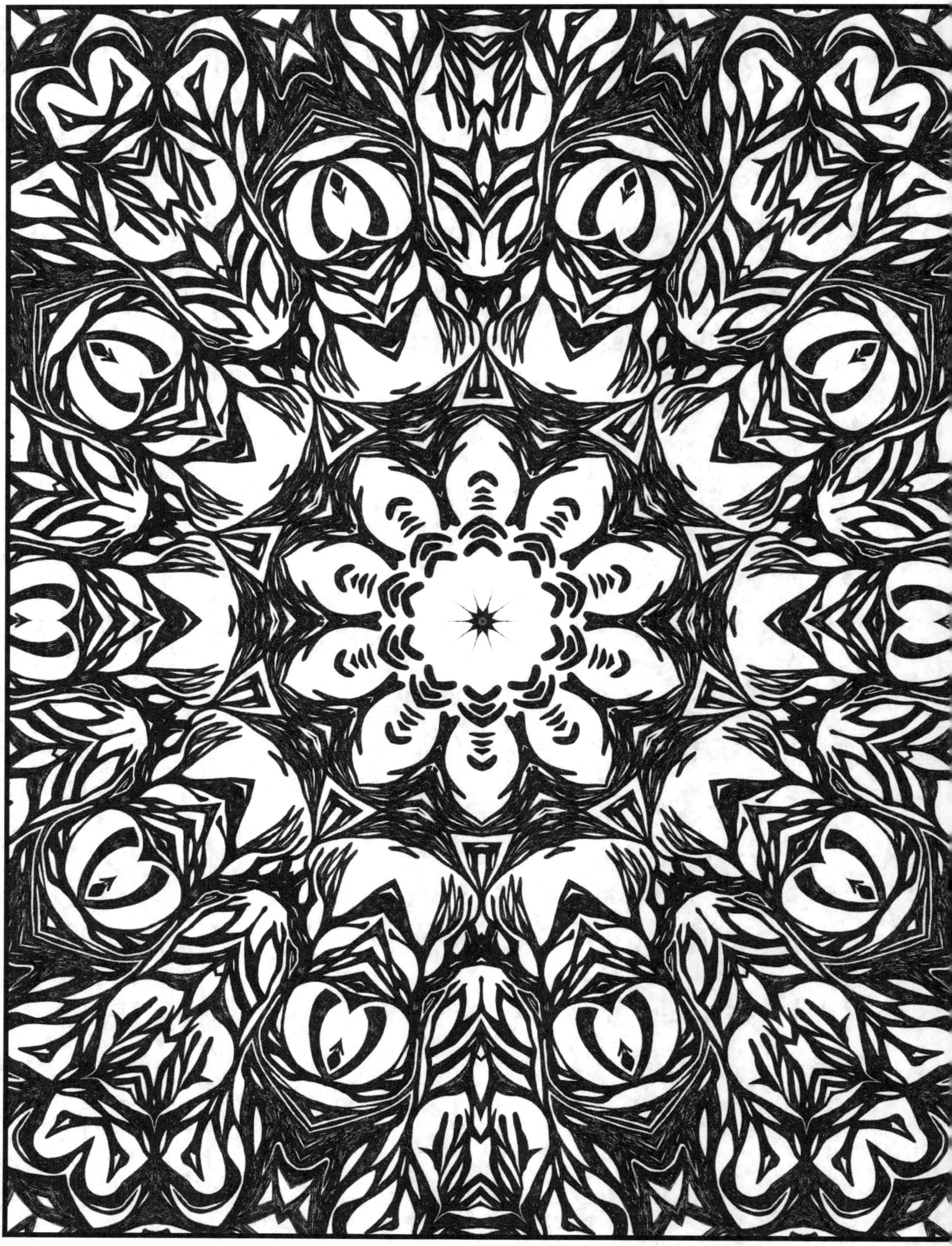

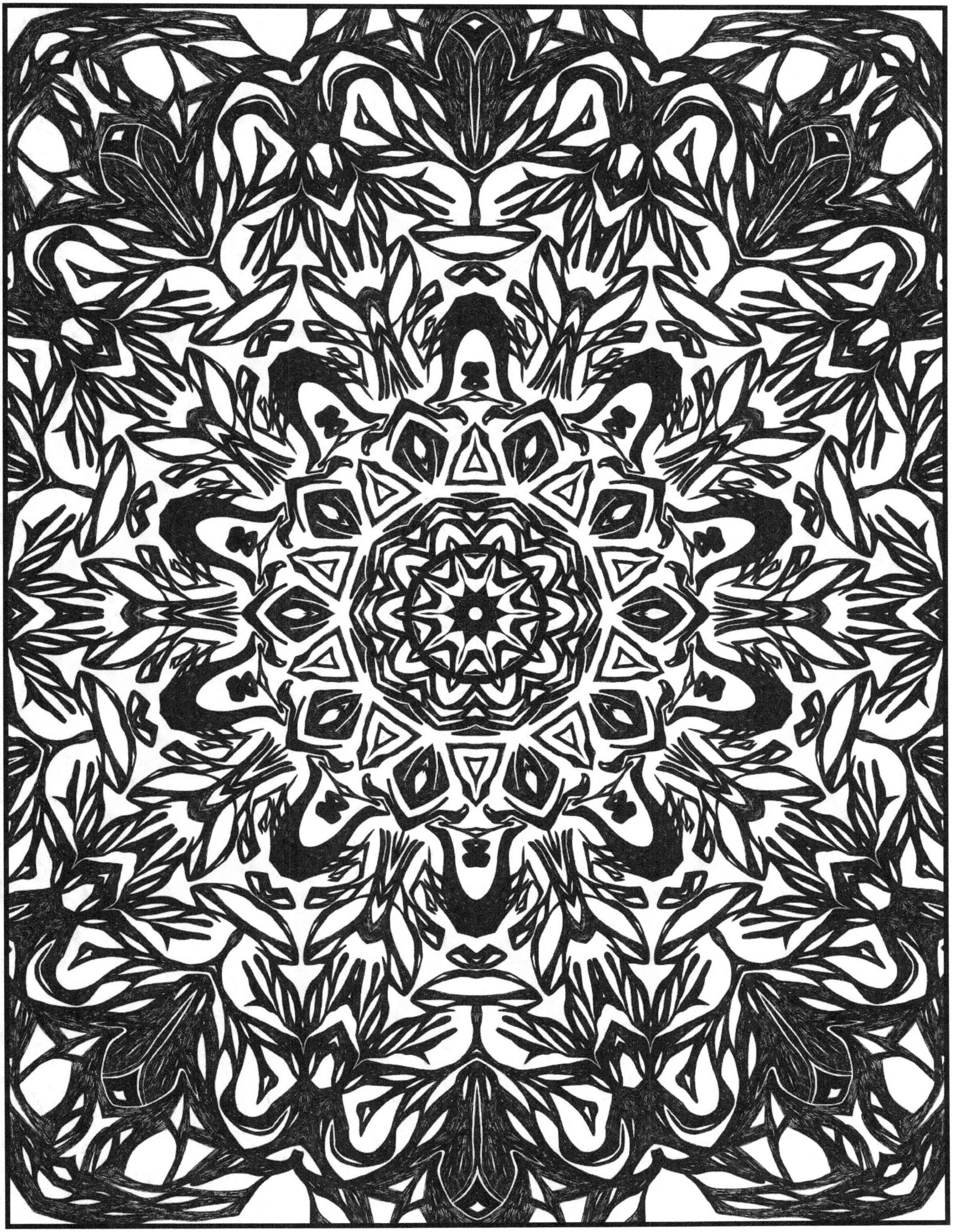

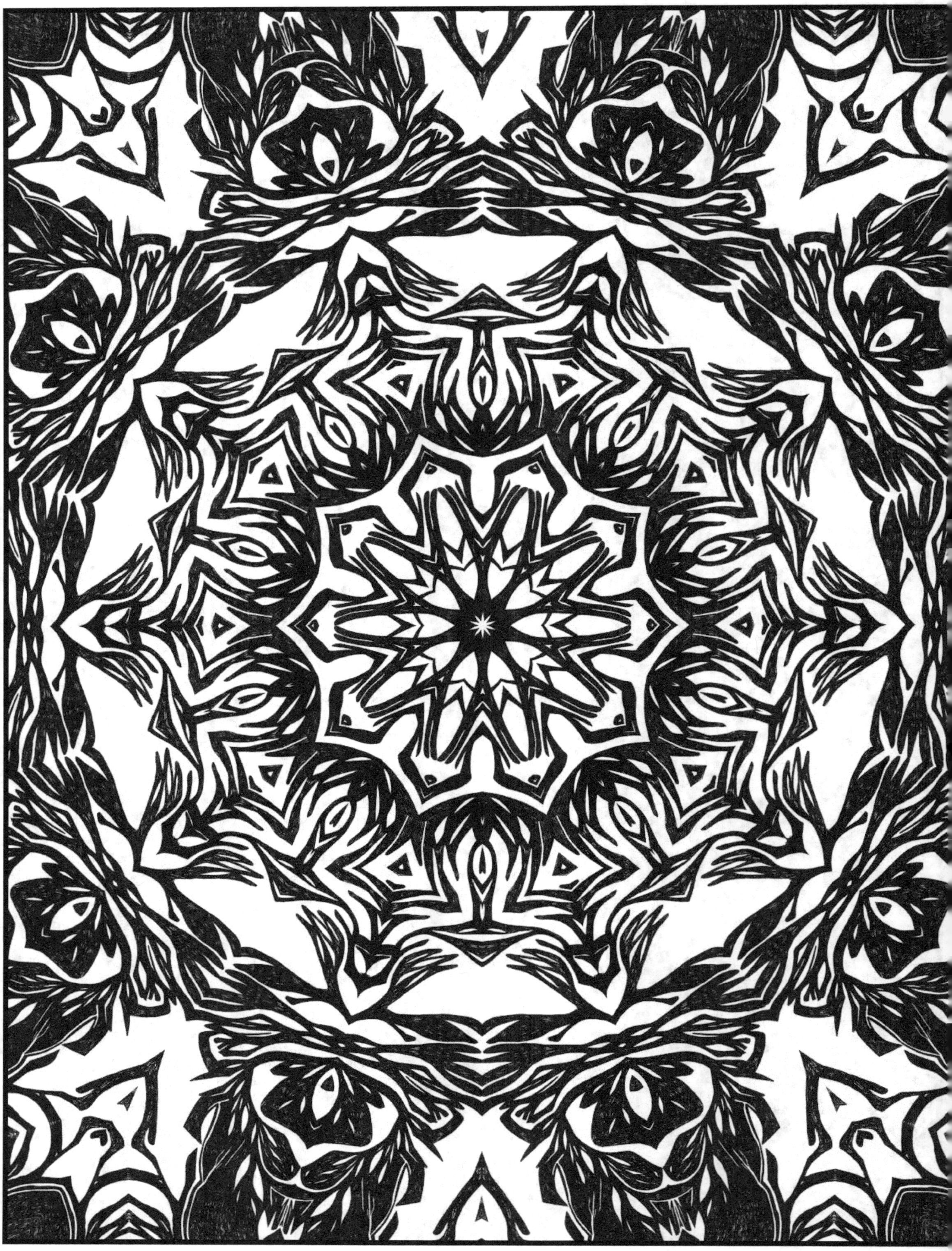

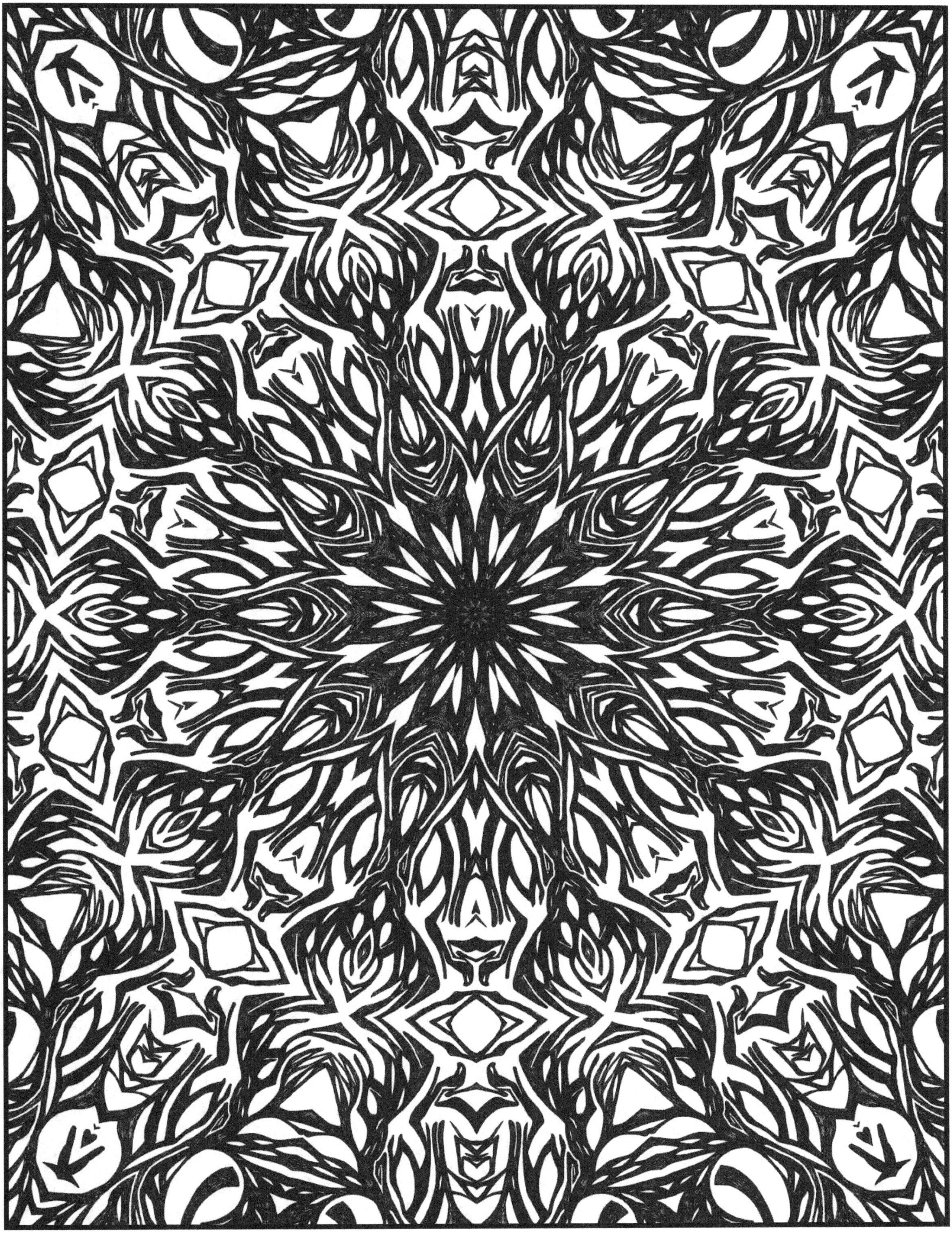

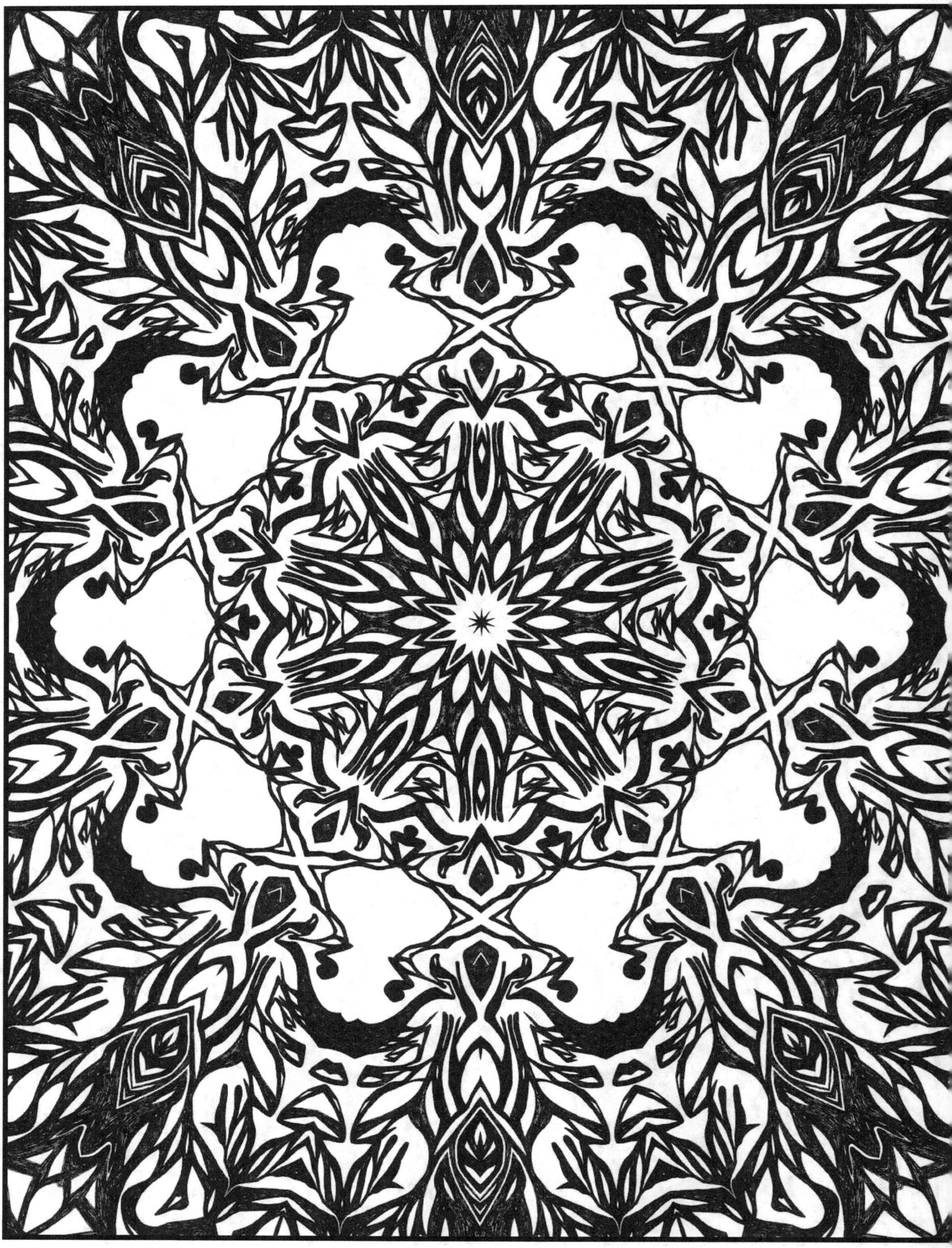

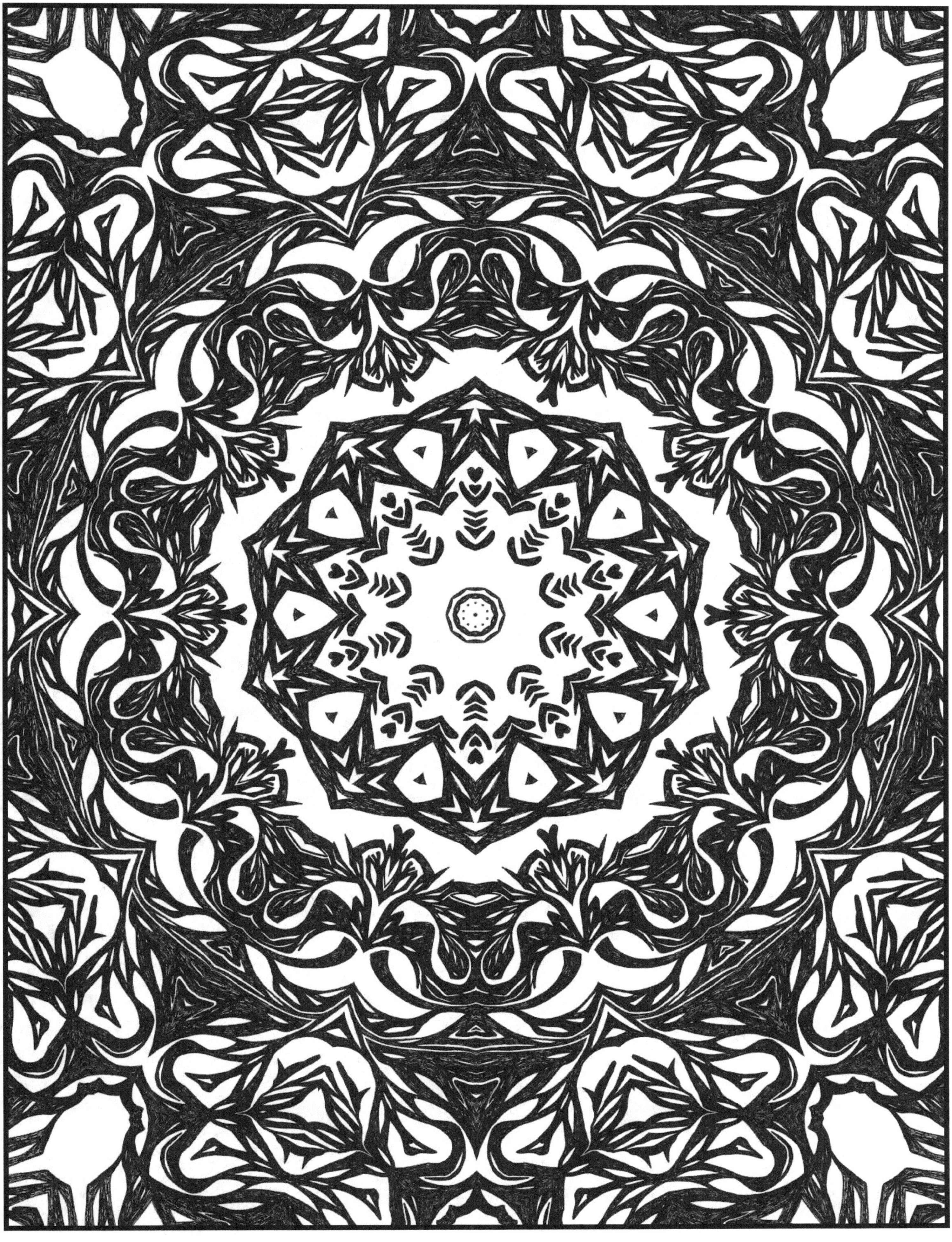

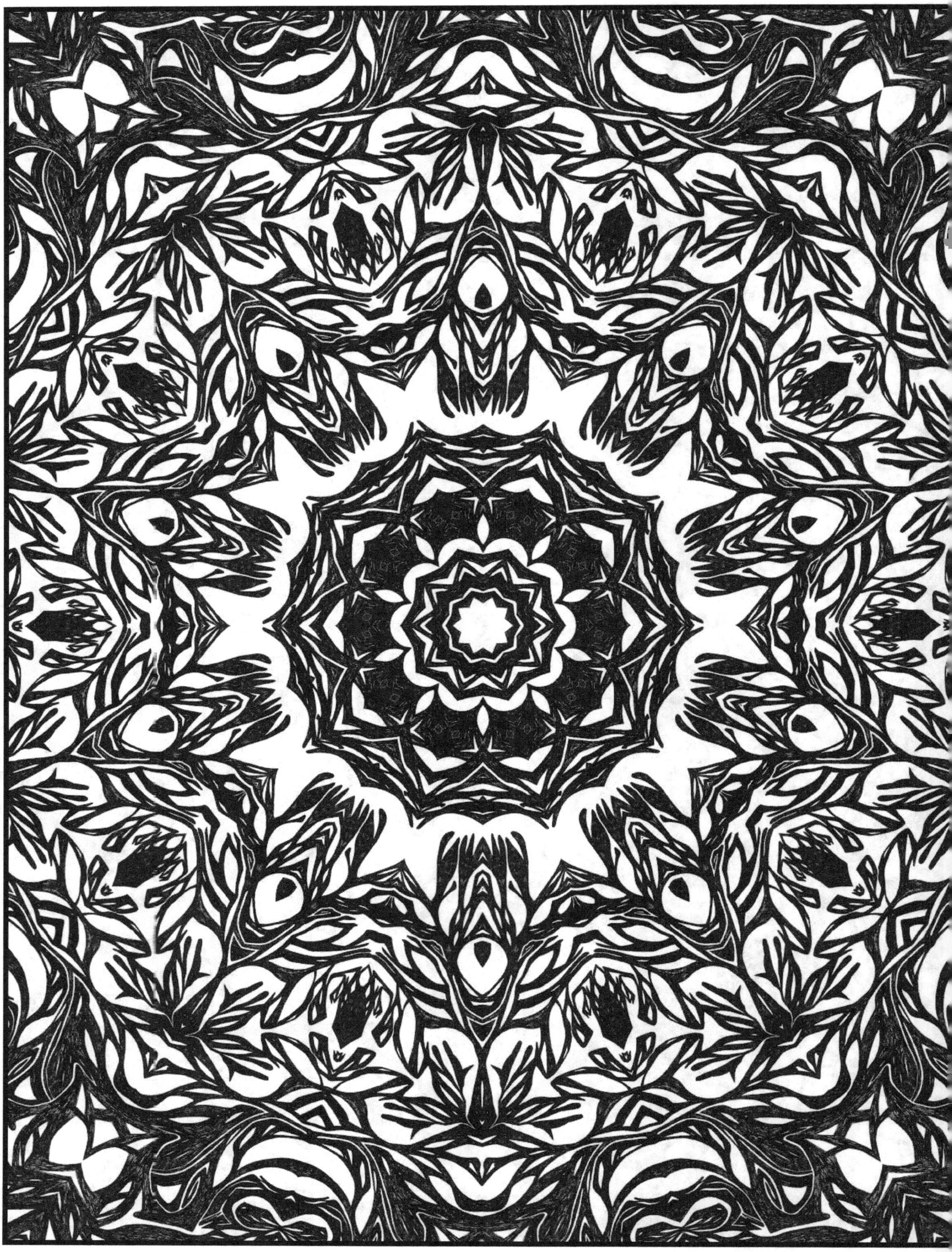

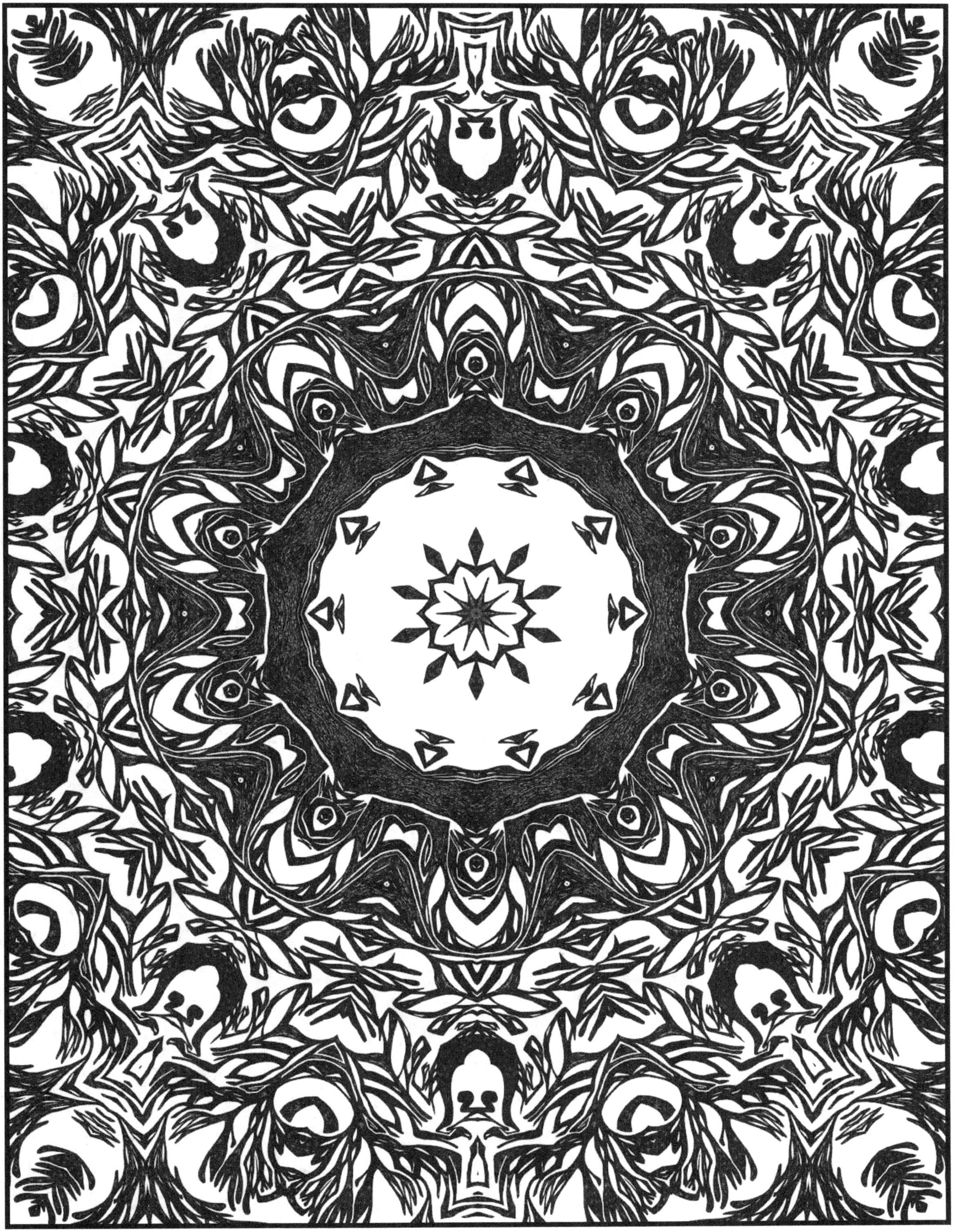

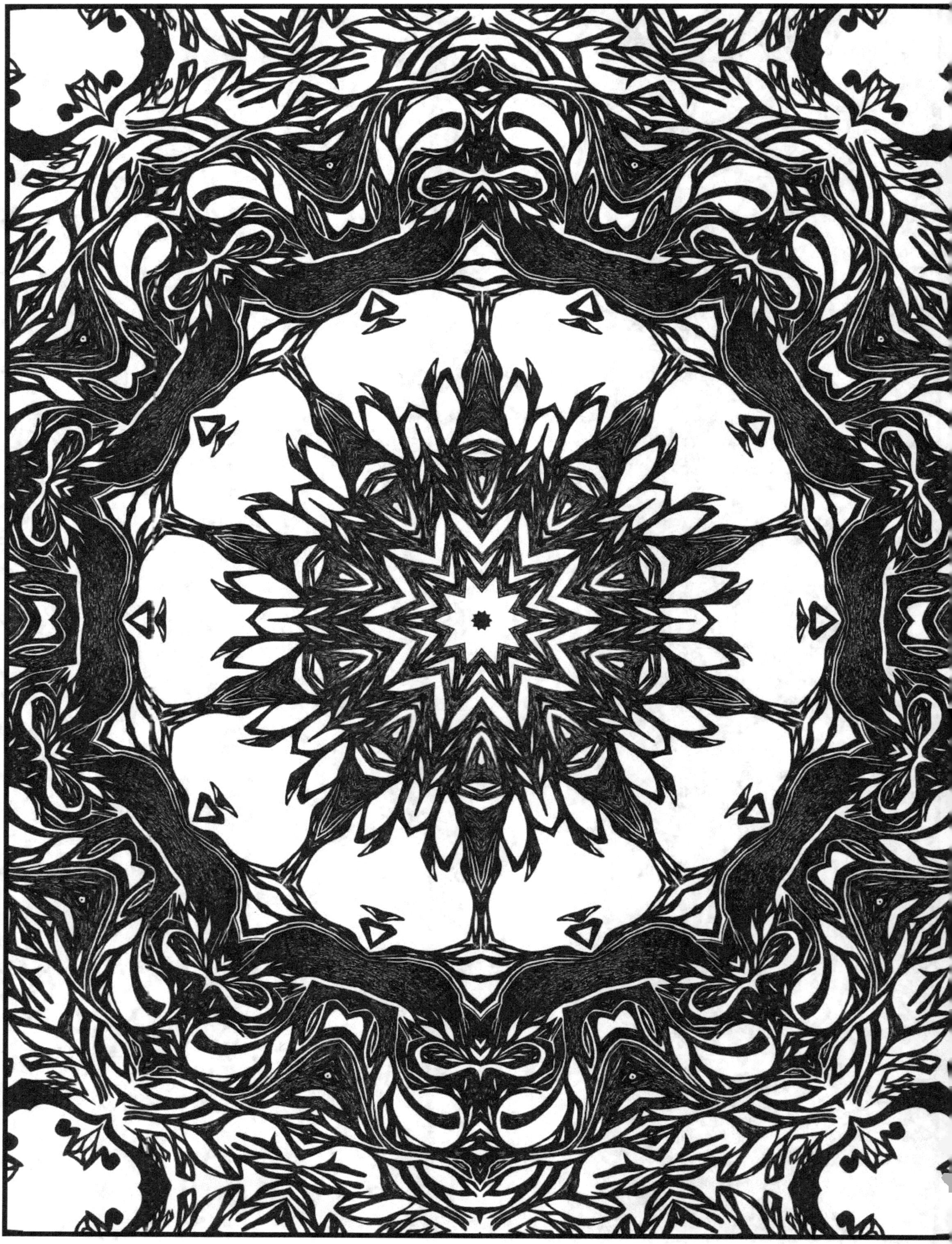

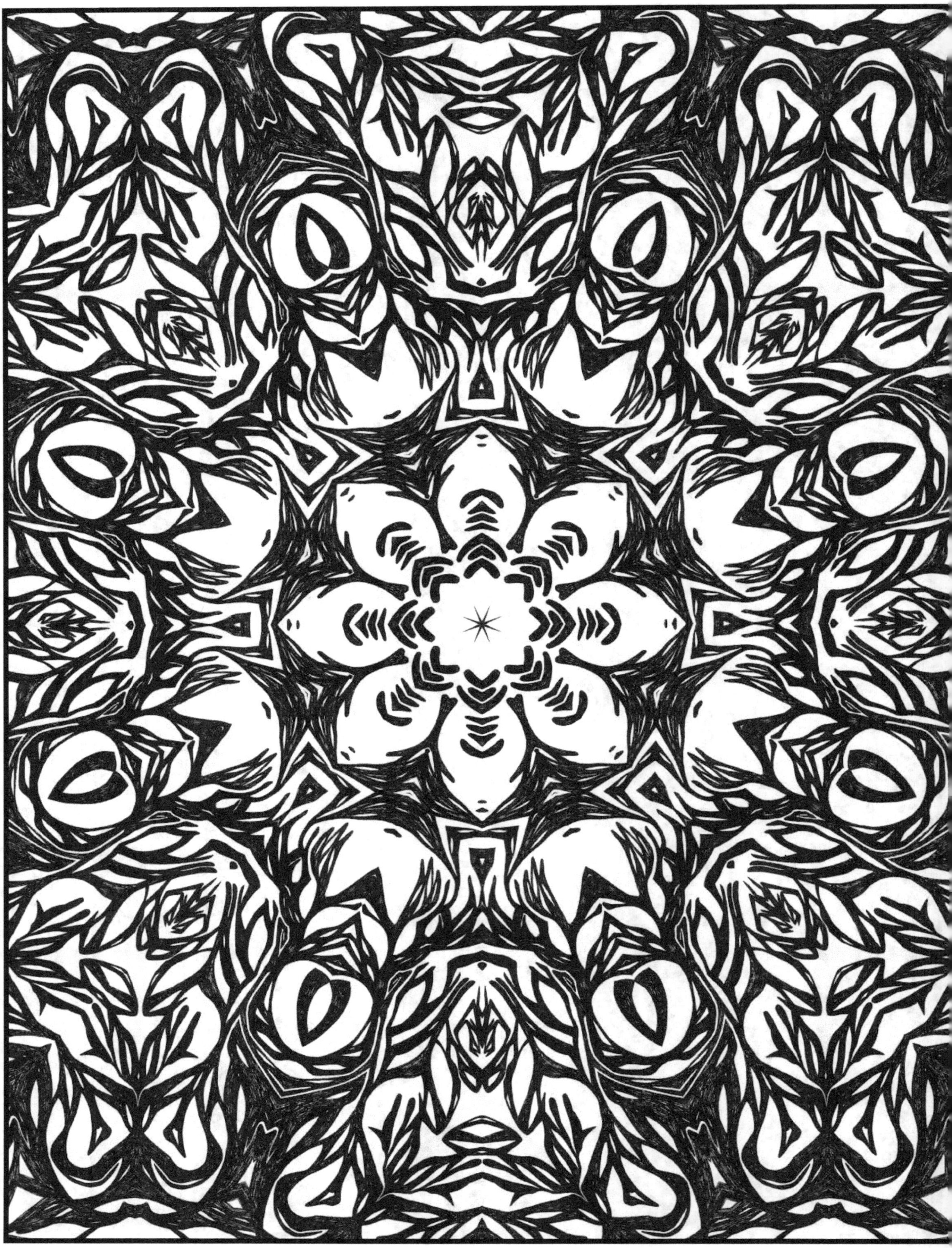

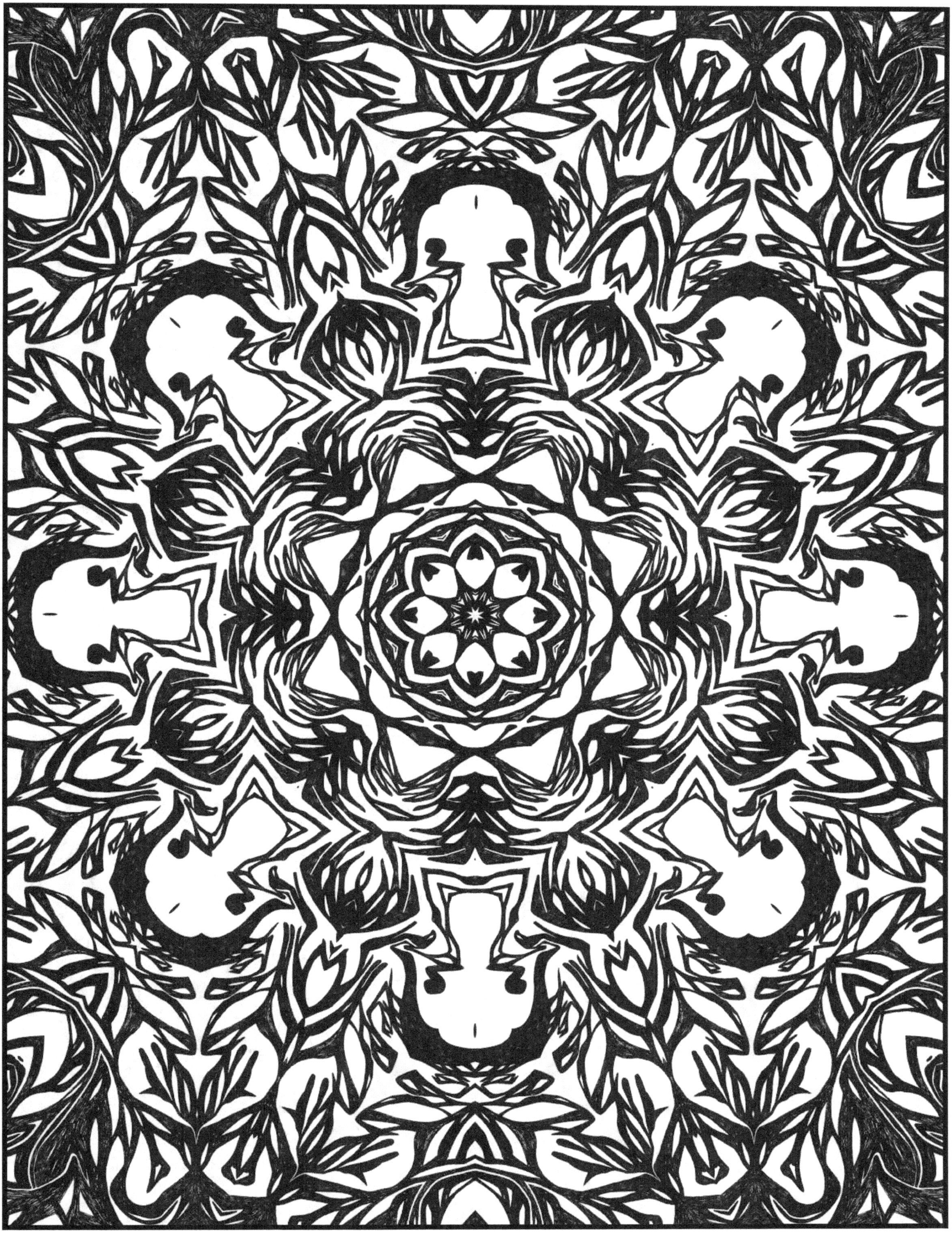

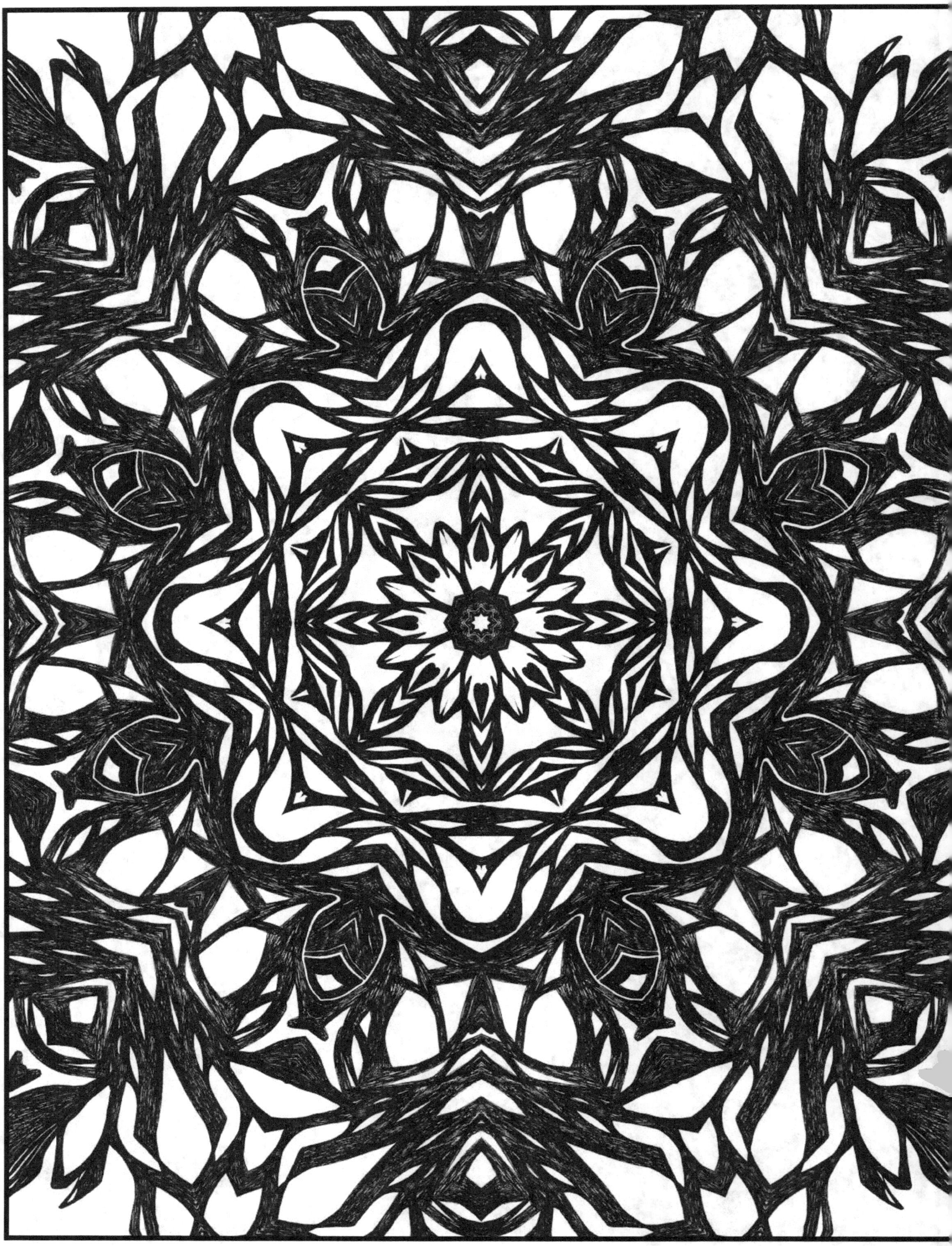

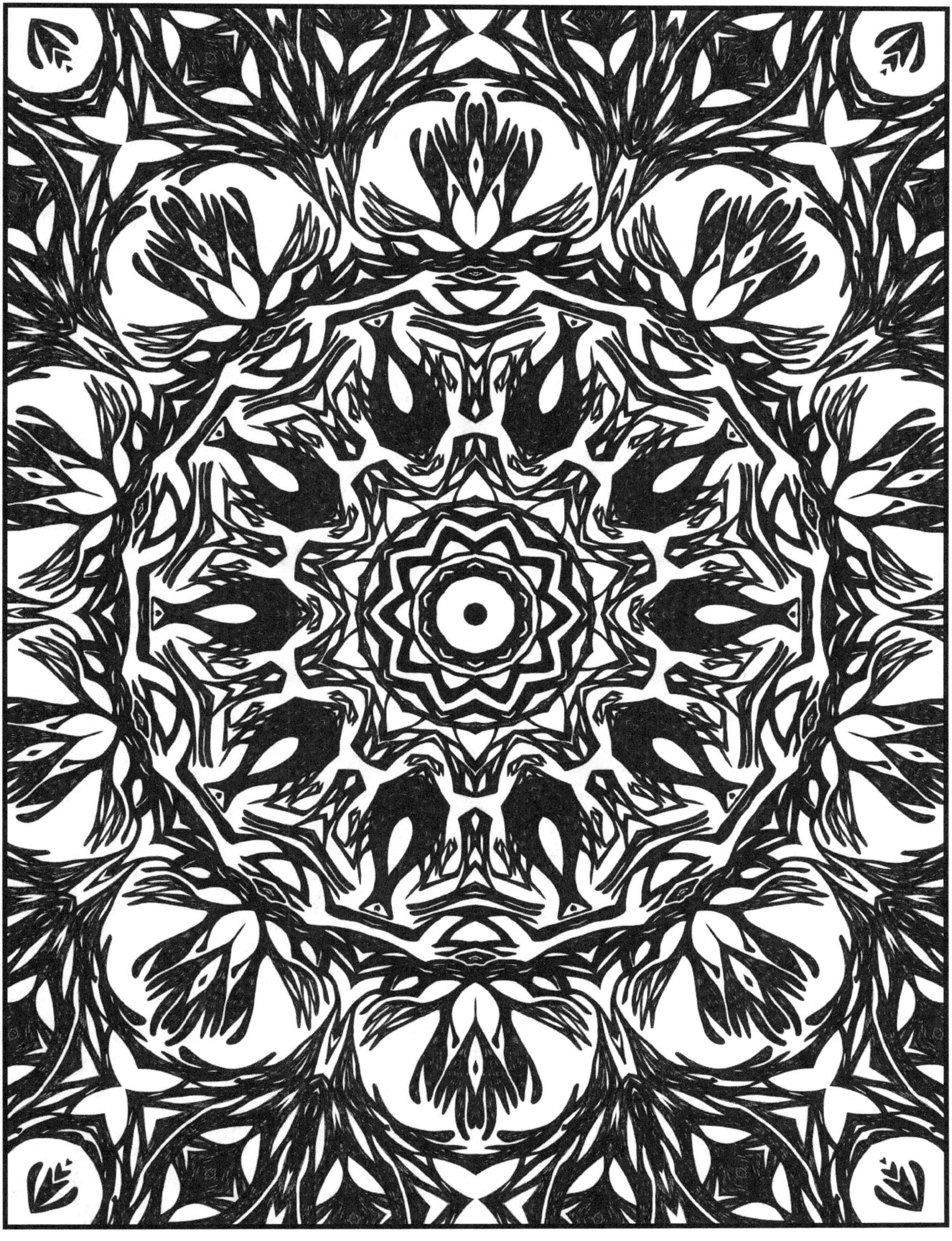

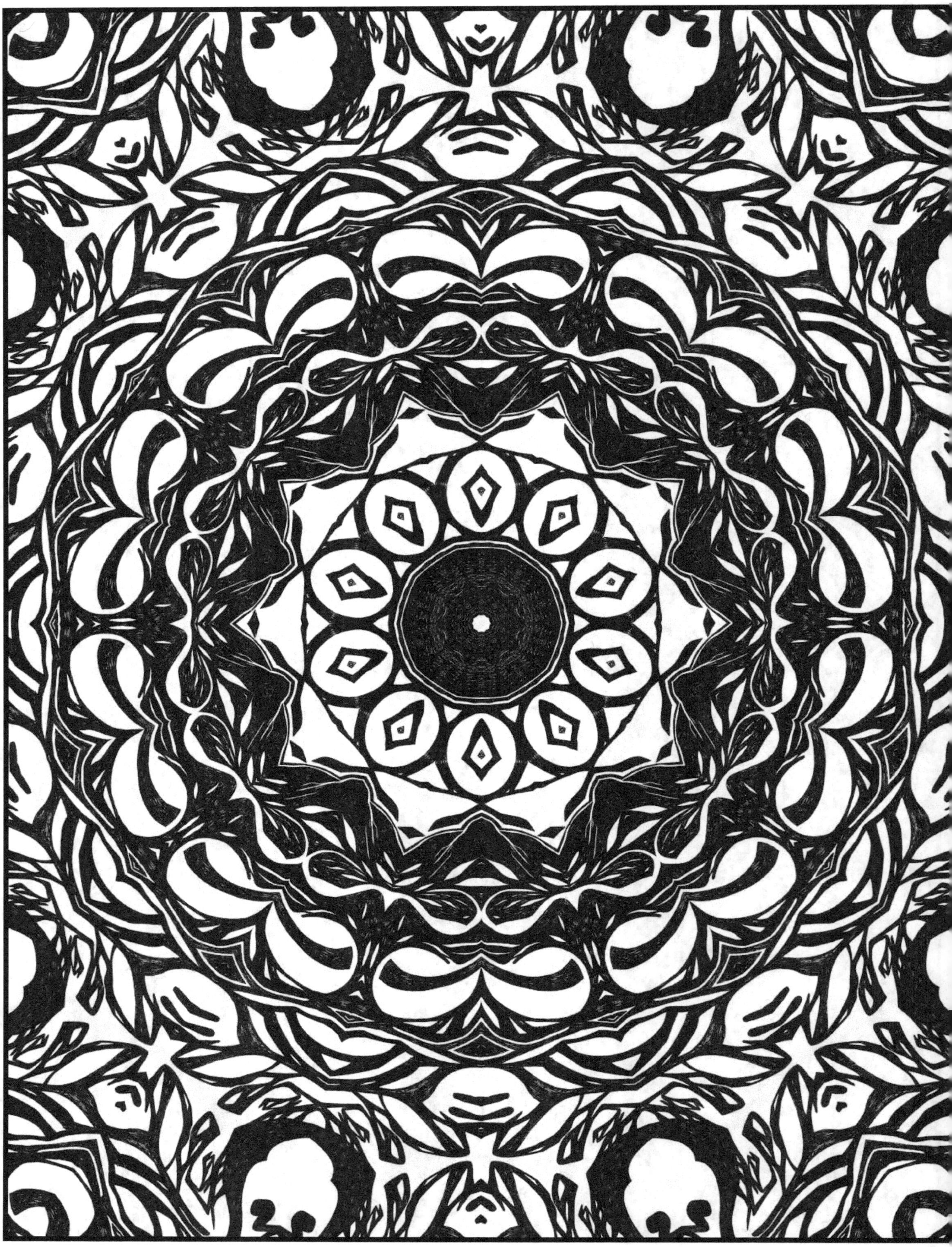

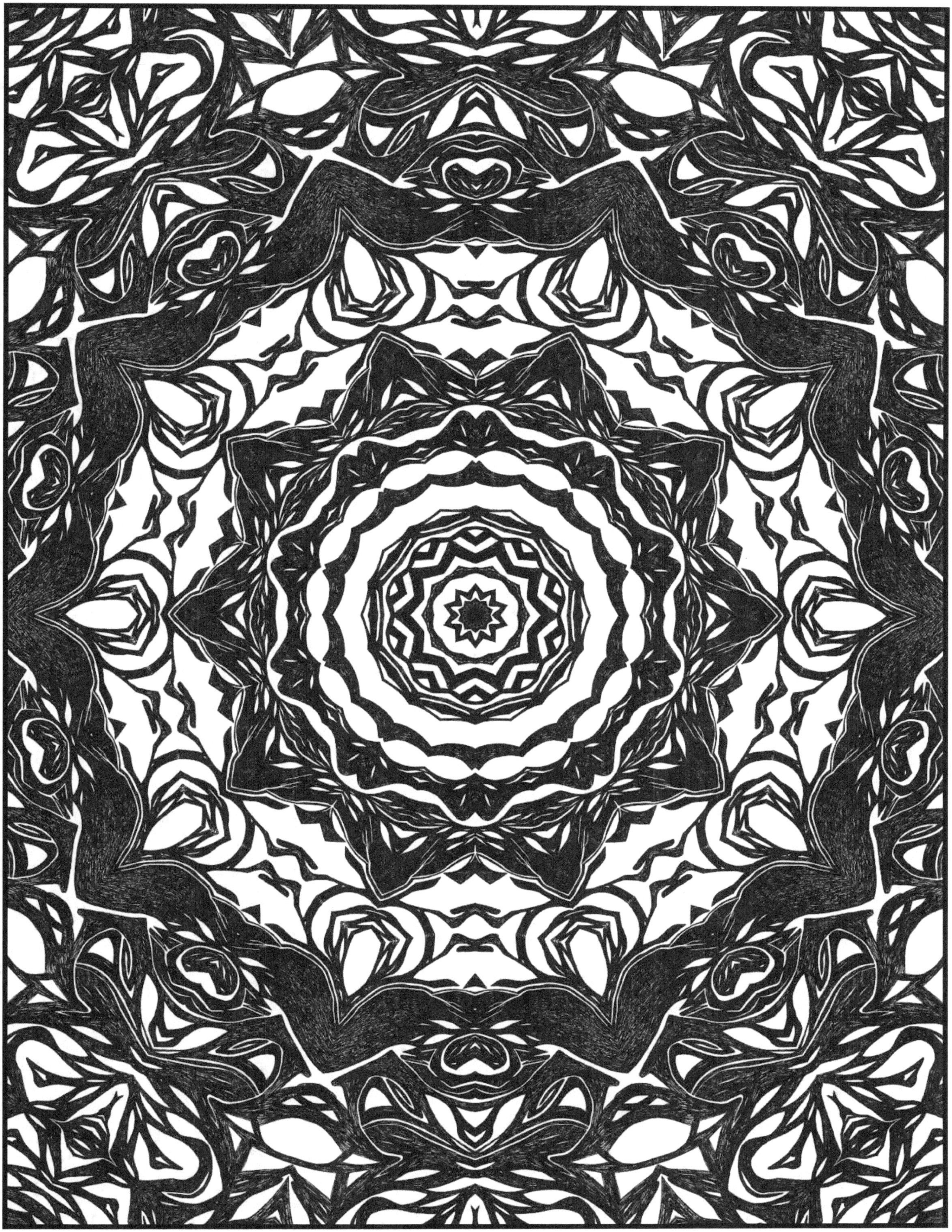

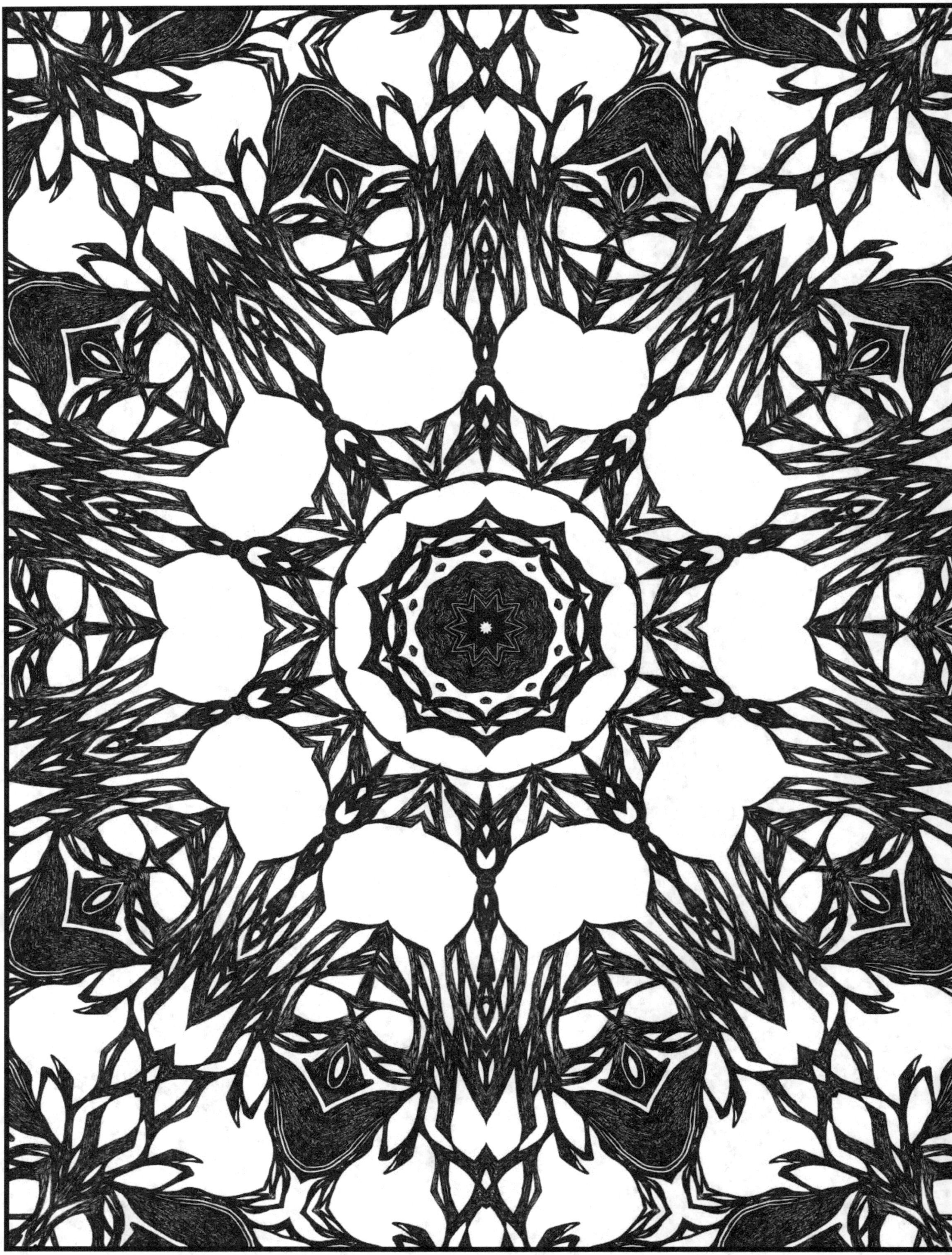

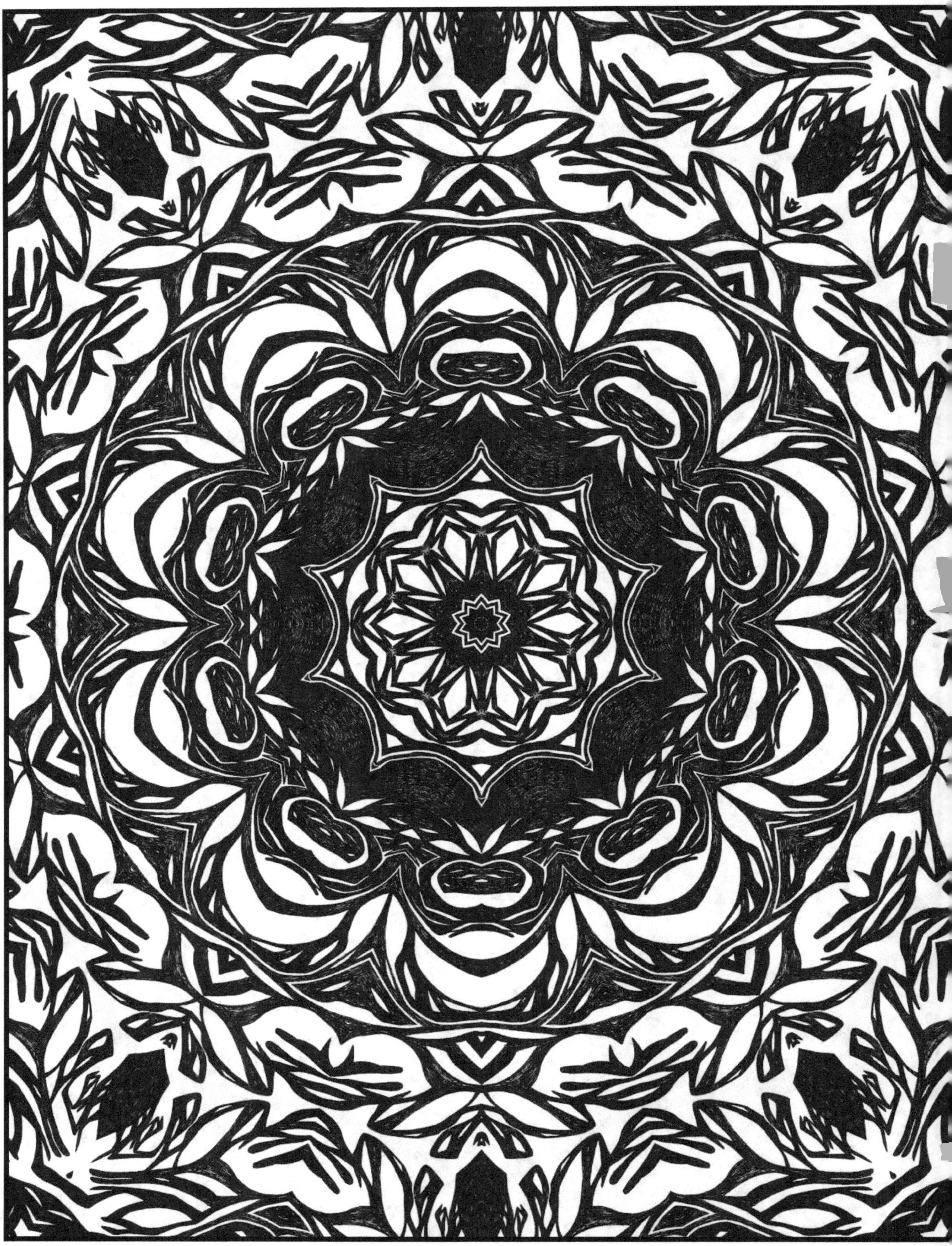

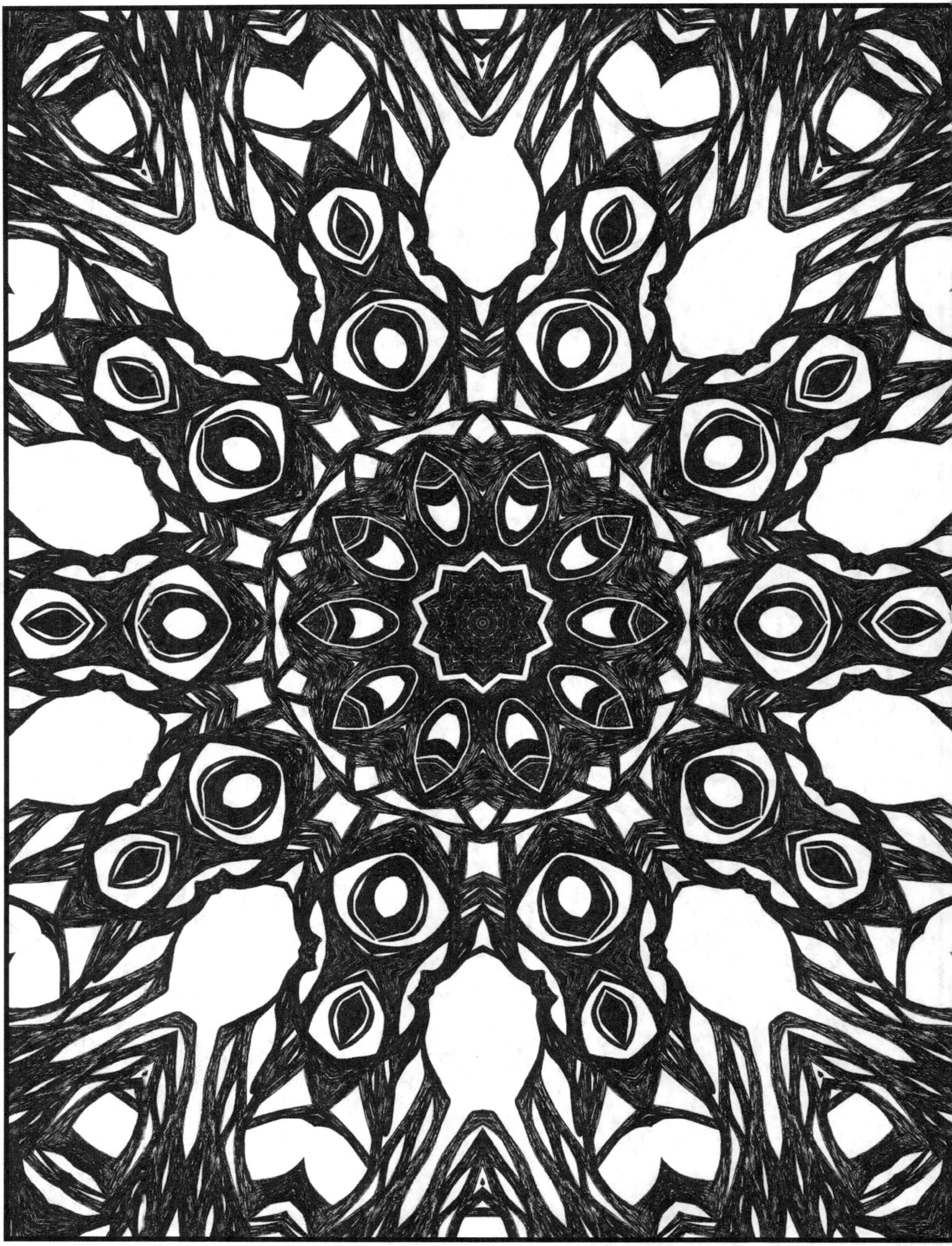

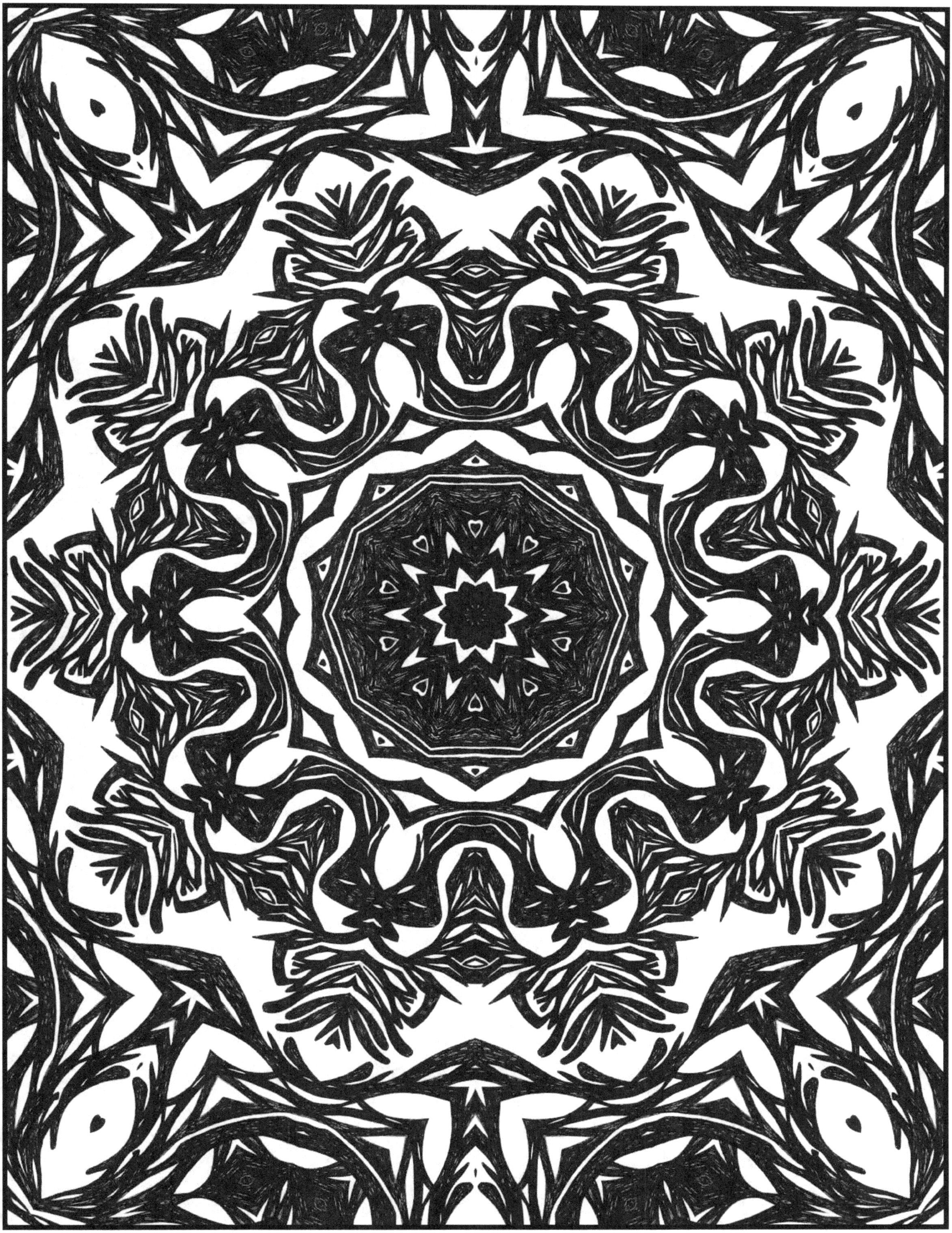

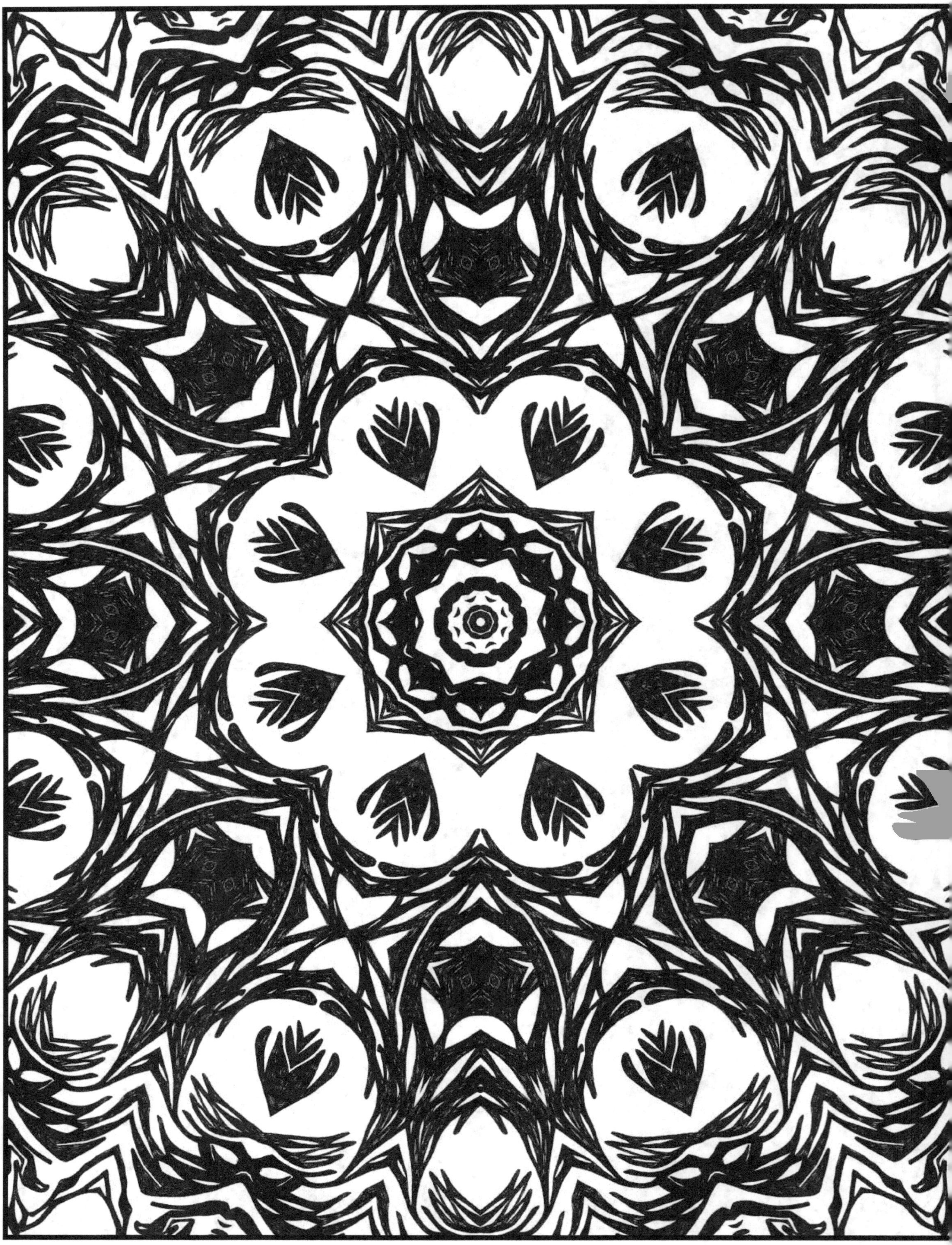

www.ingramcontent.com/pod-product-compliance
Lightning Source LLC
Chambersburg PA
CBHW082009230526
45468CB00023B/2969
* 9 7 8 1 7 2 0 9 5 3 4 4 9 *